A GUIDE TO SHIPBUILDING CONTRACTS

FIRST EDITION

BY

ALBERT LAZARUS,

LLM, IMO IMLI

Member Indian Council of Arbitration,

Member Bar council of India,

Ex Master Mariner

To my parents,
Vincent and Elizabeth

And my wonderful wife,
Anugrah,
for her support throughout this journey

Preface

Having been involved in the shipping industry for more than 20 years in different roles, I have been wanting to publish a book on the complex subject of ship building contract. I was introduced to this subject in more detail during my LLM course at IMO IMLI, Malta.

My association with Norwegian shipping companies who constantly upgraded their fleet of ships made the subject all the more interesting with first hand experience at various shipyards. The thought of the development taking place around the Indian coast and the Government of India focus on developing the maritime sector prompted me to write this book.

When I started writing this book during my visit to a famous shipyard in Korea in 2015, I noticed that there was a huge rush at the shipyard with new building orders to the full. By the end of year 2016, many of those vessels on order were launched. In the year 2017, there were hardly any orders for new building vessels. The market for new building vessels had by now substantially reduced and many of the work force laid off. This was the face of reality in this grueling, harsh industry. But after every slump the market has always rebounded and we see new players coming abreast the established ones.

Most of the ship yards that delivered vessels were in Korea, some in China and even in Vietnam. I have hardly heard of any new building vessel being delivered in Japan or Europe of late due to the obvious high costs involved. My focus is on conventional cargo vessels and not small crafts or passenger vessels keeping in view the upcoming Indian market and the Indian shipbuilding industry.

This book focuses on the Japanese SAJ form which mostly favored the ship yard as against the ship owner. To cut a balance between the shipyard and ship owner BIMCO came up with the NEWBUILDCON form of ship building contract. Due to the increase demand of vessels being built in China, the China Maritime Arbitration Commission (CMAC) has come up with a standard form Chinese ship building contract.

I would like to thank my lecturers at IMO IMLI Malta, specially Mrs. Elda Belja and the director of IMO IMLI Malta Prof. David Attard.

Albert Lazarus

ABBREVIATIONS

In order of the publication

SAJ Form - Shipbuilder's Association of Japan
NEWBUILDCON – by BIMCO, the Baltic and International Maritime Council
CMAC – China Maritime Arbitration Commission
AWES – Association of European Shipbuilders and Ship repairers
MARAD – The Maritime Administration of the United States Department of Commerce
LOA - Length overall
LOI - Letter of Intent
LBP - Length between the perpendiculars
GRT - Gross tonnage
Dwt – Deadweight
MEPC - Marine Environment Protection Committee
EEDI - Energy Efficiency Design Index
ECA - Emission Control Areas
ADR - Alternative Dispute Resolution
LSA - Life saving appliances
FFA - Fire fighting appliances
IACS - International Association of Classification Societies
IRS - Indian Register of Shipping
DNV GL - Det Norske Veritas Germanischer Lloyd
LR - Lloyd's Register
KR - Korean Register of Shipping
ABS - American Bureau of Shipping
CCS - China Classification Society
NK/ClassNK - Nippon Kaiji Kyokai
BV - Bureau Veritas
RS - Russian Maritime Register of Shipping
RINA - Registro Italiano Navale
PRS - Polish Register of Shipping
CRS - Croatian Register of Shipping
IMO - International Maritime Organisation
MEPC - Marine Environment Protection Committee
CO2 - Carbon dioxide
EEDI - Energy Efficiency Design Index
ECA - Emission Control Areas
SOx – Sulphur Oxide
NOx – Nitrous Oxide
ISO - International Standards Organization
MCR - Maximum Continuous Rating
NCR - nominal continuous rating
SOLAS - International Convention for the Safety of Life at Sea 1974, as amended
MARPOL - International Convention for the Prevention of Pollution from Ships, 1973, as modified by the Protocol of 1978 relating thereto and by the Protocol of 1997
UNCITRAL -The United Nations Commission on International Trade Law
FOC Flag of Convenience
MSC Maritime Safety Committee
NSA Norwegian Ship owner's Association
OCIMF Oil Companies International Marine Forum

ICS International Chamber of Shipping
ILO International Labour Organization
ITF International Transport Workers' Federation
ISM International Safety Management
ISPS Code The International Ship and Port Facility Security Code
PMS Planned Maintenance System
PSC Port State Control
SMS Safety Management System
STCW Standards of Training, Certification and Watch keeping
UNCLOS United Nations Convention on Law of the Seas
UMS Unmanned machinery space

LIST OF CONVENTIONS

- International Convention for the Safety of Life at Sea (SOLAS), 1974, as amended
- International Convention for the Prevention of Pollution from Ships, 1973, as modified by the Protocol of 1978 relating thereto and by the Protocol of 1997 (MARPOL 73/78)
- International Convention on Standards of Training, Certification and Watchkeeping for Seafarers (STCW) as amended, including the 1995 and 2010 Manila Amendments
- Convention on the International Regulations for Preventing Collisions at Sea (COLREG), 1972
- Convention on Facilitation of International Maritime Traffic (FAL), 1965
- International Convention on Load Lines (LL), 1966
- International Convention on Maritime Search and Rescue (SAR), 1979
- Convention for the Suppression of Unlawful Acts Against the Safety of Maritime Navigation(SUA), 1988, and Protocol for the Suppression of Unlawful Acts Against the Safety of Fixed Platforms located on the Continental Shelf (and the 2005 Protocols)
- International Convention for Safe Containers (CSC), 1972
- Convention on the International Maritime Satellite Organization (IMSO C), 1976
- The Torremolinos International Convention for the Safety of Fishing Vessels (SFV), 1977, superseded by the The 1993 Torremolinos Protocol; Cape Town Agreement of 2012 on the Implementation of the Provisions of the 1993 Protocol relating to the Torremolinos International Convention for the Safety of Fishing Vessels
- International Convention on Standards of Training, Certification and Watchkeeping for Fishing Vessel Personnel (STCW-F), 1995
- Maritime Labour Convention 2006 (MLC 2006)
- Special Trade Passenger Ships Agreement (STP), 1971 and Protocol on Space Requirements for Special Trade Passenger Ships, 1973
- International Convention Relating to Intervention on the High Seas in Cases of Oil Pollution Casualties (INTERVENTION), 1969
- Convention on the Prevention of Marine Pollution by Dumping of Wastes and Other Matter (LC), 1972 (and the 1996 London Protocol)
- International Convention on Oil Pollution Preparedness, Response and Co-operation (OPRC), 1990
- Protocol on Preparedness, Response and Co-operation to pollution Incidents by Hazardous and Noxious Substances, 2000 (OPRC-HNS Protocol)
- International Convention on the Control of Harmful Anti-fouling Systems on Ships (AFS), 2001
- International Convention for the Control and Management of Ships' Ballast Water and Sediments, 2004
- The Hong Kong International Convention for the Safe and Environmentally Sound Recycling of Ships, 2009
- International Convention on Civil Liability for Oil Pollution Damage (CLC), 1969
- 1992 Protocol to the International Convention on the Establishment of an International Fund for Compensation for Oil Pollution Damage (FUND 1992)
- Convention relating to Civil Liability in the Field of Maritime Carriage of Nuclear Material(NUCLEAR), 1971
- Athens Convention relating to the Carriage of Passengers and their Luggage by Sea (PAL), 1974
- Convention on Limitation of Liability for Maritime Claims (LLMC), 1976

- International Convention on Liability and Compensation for Damage in Connection with the Carriage of Hazardous and Noxious Substances by Sea (HNS), 1996 (and its 2010 Protocol)
- International Convention on Civil Liability for Bunker Oil Pollution Damage, 2001
- Nairobi International Convention on the Removal of Wrecks, 2007
- International Convention on Tonnage Measurement of Ships (TONNAGE), 1969
- International Convention on Salvage (SALVAGE), 1989
- The Hague Conference on Private International law Principles on Choice of Law in International Commercial Contracts
- The 1980 Rome Convention on the Law applicable to Contractual Obligations
- The United Nations Convention on Contracts for the International Sale of Goods, 1980

CASE STUDY

Stocznia Gdanska S.A. v. Latvian Shipping Co., Latreefer Inc. and Others (1998)

Man B&W Diesel S E Asia Pte and Another v PT Bumi International Tankers and Another Appeal [2004] 2 SLR(R) 300

Muscat Dhow Case, France v Great Britain, The Hague, August 8, 1905

Adler v Dickson (The Himalaya) [1954]

Stocznia Gdanska SA v Latvian Shipping Co (CA) [2002]

Rainy Sky SA and Others v Kookmin Bank

K/S A/S Bani and K/S A/S Havbulk I v. Korea Shipbuilding and Engineering Corporation

Rylands v Fletcher, 1868, L.R. 3 H.L. 330

MC Mehta v Union of India, A.I.R. 1987

Union Carbide Corporation v Union of India, A.I.R. 1992 S.C. 248

Re Anglo-Russian Merchant Traders and John Batt & Co. (London) Ltd (1917)

Website references (2018)

http://www.lawmin.nic.in

http://www.dgshipping.gov.in/Content/MerchantShippingAct

http://www.bailii.org/uk/cases/UKHL/1998/9.html

http://www.iacs.org.uk/about/members/

http://www.haguejusticeportal.net

http://www.imo.org/en/KnowledgeCentre/IndexofIMOResolutions/Maritime-Safety-Committee-(MSC)/Documents/MSC.137(76).pdf.

https://www.ocimf.org/media/60654/Guide-for-Implementation-of-Sulphur-Oxide-Exhaust-Gas-Cleaning-Systems-030816.pdf

www.ipindia.nic.in/faq-patents.htm

https://www.hcch.net/en/instruments/conventions/full-text/?cid=135

www.jus.uio.no/lm/ec.applicable.law.contracts.1980/

https://www.uncitral.org/pdf/english/texts/sales/cisg/V1056997-CISG-e-book.pdf

TABLE OF CONTENTS

INTRODUCTION

A shipbuilding contract is a complex contract as compared to the other subjects of contract laws. It is basically a contract which is the outcome of an agreement between two legal entities comprising with the usual elements of contract such as proposal, acceptance, consent, competence and consideration to have an outcome of a legal object that is the ship.

Section 2(h) of Indian Contract Act, 1872 states that 'an agreement enforceable by law is a contract'. While all contracts are agreements, all agreements are not contracts. If the agreement can be enforced by law then it will be a contract. An agreement not enforceable by law is said to be void.[1] Section 2(e) of the Act defines agreement as 'every promise and every set of promises, forming the consideration for each other, is an agreement'.

Section 10 of Indian Contract Act, 1872 states that 'all agreements are contracts if they are made by the free consent of the parties competent to contract, for a lawful consideration and with a lawful object and are not expressly declared to be void'.

Thus for a valid contract, the following elements are essential:

1. There must be intention to create legal obligation through offer and acceptance.
2. The parties must give their free consent. There must be no coercion, undue influence, fraud, misrepresentation or mistake.
3. The parties must be competent to contract. The contracting party must be a major, of sound mind and is not disqualified by law to contract.
4. There must be a lawful consideration and lawful object. It would be unlawful if it is forbidden by law, is fraudulent, or causes injury to the person or property of another, or is immoral or opposed to any public policy.

The law of sale of goods in India was governed by Chapter VII (sections 76 to 123) of the Indian Contract Act, 1872. Since the Indian Contract Act is based on the English Common Law, the law relating to the sale of goods in India therefore followed the principles of English Common Law. The Sale of Goods Act was enacted in 1930 and the above sections from Indian Contract Act were subsequently brought into the newly formed Act.

The Sale of Goods Act draws the formalities of the contract and how it is made. A contract of sale is made by an offer to buy or sell goods for a price and the acceptance of such offer. The contract may provide for the immediate delivery of the goods or immediate payment of the price of both, or for the delivery or payment by installments, or that the delivery or payment or both shall be postponed.[2]

The subject matter of contract provides whether the goods exist or they are for future goods. The goods which form the subject of a contract of sale may be either existing goods, owned or

---

[1] Indian Contract Act, 1872, Section 2(g).
[2] Sale of Goods Act, 1930, Chapter II, Section 5.1.

possessed by the seller, or future goods.[3] Where by a contract of sale the seller purports to effect a present sale of future goods, the contract operates as an agreement to sell the goods.[4]

The vessel under construction is a huge project, involving numerous technical persons and materials. It begins with the design stage, blueprint and then goes The ship construction is a huge project which involves various stages. From naval architects designing the ship, to various expert welders joining each completed section of the vessel, to mounting various equipment. All equipment are not manufactured by the yard. In fact, the yard sub contracts the installation of various equipment such as diesel generators, boilers, radars, navigational equipment to various manufacturers and their licensed contractors. Enormous amount of funds will be needed in the beginning which the yard invests in and will therefore ensure that it gets the funds at various stages of the construction of the vessel. Thus the question arises, is it a contract of sale or is it a contract for works and materials.

It is well settled in English law that though the shipbuilding contract is for construction of the vessel, it is in law a contract for the sale of goods.

Since *McDougall* these features have been recognised in two House of Lords decisions, *Hyundai Heavy Industries Co.* v. *Papadopoulos and Others* (1980)[5] and *Stocznia Gdanska S.A.* v. *Latvian Shipping Co., Latreefer Inc. and Others* (1998),[6] which have cast some doubt on the traditional categorisation of shipbuilding contracts as pure sale contracts.[7]

In both *Hyundai* and *Stocznia Gdanska* cases, it was held that the shipbuilding contract was not only a contract of sale but was also a contract for the design and construction of the vessel.

The complexity arises due to the nature of the contractual elements.

Let us split the contractual elements in below nutshell

1. Description and class
2. Price and payment
3. Adjustment of price
4. Plans and Drawings
5. Supervision and inspection
6. Modifications, changes and extras
7. Trials
8. Delivery
9. Delays and extension / Force Majeure
10. Warranties

---

[3] Ibid, Section 6.1.
[4] Ibid, Section 6.3.
[5] [1980] 2 Lloyd's Rep. 1.
[6] [1998] 1 Lloyd's Rep. 609.
[7] Curtis Simon; The Law of Shipbuilding Contracts, Fourth edition, Informa Law from Routledge, Oxon. U.K., 2012, p. 2.

11. Rescission by BUYER
12. BUYER'S default
13. Insurance
14. Dispute and Arbitration
15. Assignment
16. Copyright, trademark
17. Notices
18. Guarantee

A shipbuilding contract will cover the above elements. There are standard contract forms available such as mentioned below:

SAJ Form - Shipbuilder's Association of Japan

NEWBUILDCON – by BIMCO, the Baltic and International Maritime Council

CMAC – China Maritime Arbitration Commission

AWES – Association of European Shipbuilders and Ship repairers

The Norwegian Shipowners Association and Norwegian Shipbuilders Association

MARAD – The Maritime Administration of the United States Department of Commerce

The basis of this publication is the SAJ Form.

PREAMBLE

THIS CONTRACT, made this ……….....day of , ……………….. 19 (sic)……………. , by and between……………………………………………………………………………………………... , a corporation
organised and existing under the laws of Japan, having its principal office at
………………………………………………………………………………………………………
…………., Japan (hereinafter called the ''BUILDER''), the party of the first part, and
……………………………………………………………………………………………., a corporation
organised
and existing under the laws of………………………………………………………………………
having its principal office at …………………………………………………………….(hereinafter
called the ''BUYER''), the party of the second part,

WITNESSETH:
In consideration of the mutual covenants herein contained, the BUILDER agrees to build, launch, equip and complete at its………………………….....(hereinafter called the ''SHIPYARD'') and sell and deliver to the BUYER one (1)…………………………………….more fully described in Article 1 hereof (hereinafter called the ''VESSEL''), and the BUYER agrees to purchase and take delivery of the VESSEL from the BUILDER and to pay for the same, all upon the terms and conditions hereinafter set forth.

ARTICLE I – DESCRIPTION AND CLASS

1. Description:

The VESSEL shall have the BUILDER'S Hull No. .... and shall be constructed, equipped and completed in accordance with the provisions of this Contract, and the Specifications and the General Arrangement Plan (herein collectively called the "Specifications") signed by each of the parties hereto for identification and attached hereto and made an integral part hereof.

2. Dimensions and Characteristics:

Any and all payments by the BUYER to the BUILDER under this Contract shall be made in non-resident convertible free Japanese Yen.

Length, overall...

Length, between perpendiculars..

Breadth, moulded..

Depth, moulded
....

Designed loaded draft, moulded Gross tonnage...

Propelling Machinery
....

Deadweight, guaranteed
....

Trial speed, guaranteed..

Fuel consumption, guaranteed...

The details of the above particulars as well as the definitions and method of measurements and calculations are as indicated in the Specifications.

3. Classification, Rules and Regulations:

The VESSEL, including its machinery, equipment and outfittings shall be constructed in accordance with the rules (the edition and amendments thereto being in force as of the date of this Contract) of and under special survey of........... (herein called the "Classification Society"), and shall be distinguished in the register by the symbol of...
Decisions of the Classification Society as to compliance or non-compliance with the classification shall be final and binding upon both parties hereto. The VESSEL shall also comply with the rules, regulations and requirements of other regulatory bodies as described in the Specifications in effect as of the date of this Contract.

All fees and charges incidental to the classification and with respect to compliance with the above referred rules, regulations and requirements shall be for account of the BUILDER.

4. Subcontracting:

The BUILDER may, at its sole discretion [*sic*] and responsibility, subcontract any portion of the construction work of the VESSEL.

5. Registration:

The VESSEL shall be registered by the BUYER at its own cost and expense under the laws of .... with its home port of .... at the time of its delivery and acceptance hereunder.

ARTICLE I – EXPLANATION

Description

Regarding the project and the vessel, as mentioned in the preamble, it clearly refers to Article 1 as to what the buyer and the builder agree upon. Article 1 fairly gives a description as to the intention of the buyer and the builder. It is general in nature and more details will be found later in the subsequent parts of the contract. It is obvious that the vessel name at this stage would not have been decided and hence the vessel would be assigned by the builder a Hull number. This is a common practice followed by shipyard. This Hull number will henceforth be used for all purposes to later identify the vessel in all respects. In certain countries like Germany and Italy, it is possible to register a vessel under construction and here the Hull number will be used that is assigned to the vessel under construction.

The Indian Merchant shipping Act, 1958, Part I Preliminary, Section 3(55) states that "vessel" includes any ship, boat, sailing vessel, or other description of vessel used in navigation.[8]

In *Stocznia Gdanska S.A.* v. *Latvian Shipping Co., Latreefer Inc. and Others (1998)*[9], Stocznia Gdanska S.A., the plaintiffs in the proceedings were Polish shipbuilders (yard or seller) who contracted to build the ships for Latreefers Inc., a Liberian company which was a wholly owned subsidiary of Latvian Shipping Co (buyer or purchaser). There were six shipbuilding contracts dated 11 September 1992, each for the construction of a single refrigerated vessel (commonly known as a reefer vessel).

---

[8] http://www.dgshipping.gov.in/Content/MerchantShippingAct

[9] [1998] 1 All ER 883,
[1998] WLR 574,
[1998] 1 WLR 574,
[1998] UKHL 9
URL: *http://www.bailii.org/uk/cases/UKHL/1998/9.html*

Under each of the contracts, the yard undertook to "design, build, complete and deliver" the vessel, property in the vessel not passing to the buyers until delivery. In 1992 work began on vessels 1 and 2. As per the yard the design, ordering and construction work was carried out during 1992 and 1993 pursuant to all six contracts, meaning on all 6 vessels; but however apart from work carried out in the course of laying keels for vessels 1 and 2 nothing else was done for vessels 3, 4, 5 and 6. As per terms of the contract, the first instalments of the price for all six vessels were duly paid.

In July 1993 agents for the buyers raised queries as to the price payable under all six contracts, and then in October 1993 drew attention to problems in obtaining finance for the vessels. There followed a specific proposal for a 20 per cent. reduction in the price for each vessel, together with a five-year deferral of payment of $4m. of the new reduced price and delayed delivery of all the vessels, both of which would have disrupted the yard's cash flow and work programme. It was said that this proposal was due to a downturn in the reefer market; but it is the yard's case (though this is not admitted by the buyers) that the market was already in downturn when both sets of contracts were placed in late 1992 and early 1993. Following further meetings, the buyers' agent informed the yard by letter dated 3 December 1993 that, although the buyers wanted the vessels, taking delivery of them might be impossible.

On the same day, 3 December 1993, the keel of vessel 1 was laid, and a keel laying notice was served on the buyers. However, the second instalment for vessel 1 was not paid, and the yard then served on the buyers a notice rescinding the contract under clause 5.05. The same happened with vessel 2. The keel was laid on 9 March 1993, and a keel laying notice was served; but the second instalment for this vessel too was not paid, and again the yard served a notice rescinding the contract under clause 5.05.

There followed a series of controversial events, as the yard sought to take advantage of the keels laid for vessels 1 and 2 in order to trigger the second instalments, first for vessels 3 and 4, and then for vessels 5 and 6. The purpose of the yard in doing this was plainly to secure accrued rights to the second instalments for all four of these vessels, thereby putting itself in a stronger financial position than it would have been in if it only had a right to claim damages. At all events, the keels which had originally been laid in connection with the contracts for vessels 1 and 2 were simply renumbered for vessels 3 and 4, and similarly done for vessels 5 and 6. The second instalments for these vessels were not paid, and the yard gave notice rescinding the contracts for the vessels under clause 5.05. Whether the yard was entitled to act in this way constituted an important issue in the litigation.

Dimensions and Characteristics

The principal dimensions of the vessel will be clearly laid out. The BUYER will specify the Length overall (LOA)[10], Length between the perpendiculars (LBP)[11], moulded breadth[12],

---

[10] LOA - Length of vessel taken over all extremities.
[11] LBP - The length between the forward and aft perpendiculars measured along the summer load line.
[12] Moulded breadth - Measured at the midship section is the maximum moulded breadth of the ship.

moulded depth[13], moulded Gross tonnage (GRT)[14], Propelling Machinery, guaranteed Deadweight[15], guaranteed Trial speed, guaranteed Fuel consumption. The dimensions are basically influenced by the amount of cargo that the vessel will carry. The vessel will also be required to trade in areas that are to be accessed through the Panama Canal or the Suez Canal or the Northern latitudes. The dimensions will be so designed so as to ensure smooth passage in such areas. The details of all the particulars, their definitions as well as the method of measurements and calculations would be indicated in the Specifications.

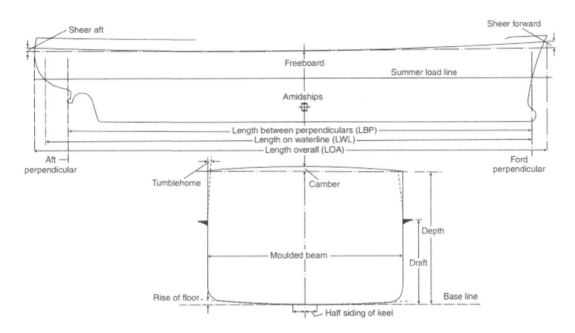

Principal ship dimensions[16]

If the specifications are not met then what are the remedies to the buyer. We will see in Article III, that there are terms of adjustment to the agreed contract price for the breach of the guaranteed standards. This will entitle the buyer to claim liquidated damages and in worst case even rescind the contract.

Classification, Rules and Regulations

---

[13] Moulded depth - Measured from the base line to the heel of the upper deck beam at the ship's side amidships.

[14] GRT - Gross tonnage is a measure of the internal capacity of the ship and net tonnage is intended to give an idea of the earning or useful capacity of the ship.

[15] Dwt - Deadweight is the difference between the lightweight and loaded displacement, i.e. it is the weight of cargo plus weights of fuel, stores, water ballast, fresh water, crew and passengers, and baggage.

[16] D.J. Eyres; Ship Construction, Fifth edition, Butterworth Heinemann, Oxford. U.K., 2001, p. 12.

The buyer selects the classification society. It is a non-governmental organisation. There are standard classification societies which are members of the International Association of Classification Societies (IACS) which is based in London. The role of the classification society is to establish and maintain technical standards for the construction and operation of the vessel. They will usually set up an office with representative, surveyors at the yard. The surveyor will inspect the works as they progress and will point out any non-compliance to the buyer's representative and the yard immediately or during their daily meetings. The main objective is to ultimately have the vessel built for the intended operations and trade. They will ensure that there is compliance with the International Maritime Organisation (IMO) standards, Flag State standards, rules, regulations and requirements of other regulatory bodies as described in the Specifications.

The following is a list of International Maritime Organisation (IMO) conventions, protocols with amendments that will be complied depending on the type, particulars and trade of vessel :

Key IMO Conventions[17]

- International Convention for the Safety of Life at Sea (SOLAS), 1974, as amended
- International Convention for the Prevention of Pollution from Ships, 1973, as modified by the Protocol of 1978 relating thereto and by the Protocol of 1997 (MARPOL)
- International Convention on Standards of Training, Certification and Watchkeeping for Seafarers (STCW) as amended, including the 1995 and 2010 Manila Amendments

Other conventions relating to maritime safety and security and ship/port interface

- Convention on the International Regulations for Preventing Collisions at Sea (COLREG), 1972
- Convention on Facilitation of International Maritime Traffic (FAL), 1965
- International Convention on Load Lines (LL), 1966
- International Convention on Maritime Search and Rescue (SAR), 1979
- Convention for the Suppression of Unlawful Acts Against the Safety of Maritime Navigation(SUA), 1988, and Protocol for the Suppression of Unlawful Acts Against the Safety of Fixed Platforms located on the Continental Shelf (and the 2005 Protocols)
- International Convention for Safe Containers (CSC), 1972
- Convention on the International Maritime Satellite Organization (IMSO C), 1976
- The Torremolinos International Convention for the Safety of Fishing Vessels (SFV), 1977, superseded by the The 1993 Torremolinos Protocol; Cape Town Agreement of 2012 on the Implementation of the Provisions of the 1993 Protocol relating to the Torremolinos International Convention for the Safety of Fishing Vessels
- International Convention on Standards of Training, Certification and Watchkeeping for Fishing Vessel Personnel (STCW-F), 1995

---

[17] http://www.imo.org/en/About/Conventions/ListOfConventions

- Special Trade Passenger Ships Agreement (STP), 1971 and Protocol on Space Requirements for Special Trade Passenger Ships, 1973

Other conventions relating to prevention of marine pollution

- International Convention Relating to Intervention on the High Seas in Cases of Oil Pollution Casualties (INTERVENTION), 1969
- Convention on the Prevention of Marine Pollution by Dumping of Wastes and Other Matter (LC), 1972 (and the 1996 London Protocol)
- International Convention on Oil Pollution Preparedness, Response and Co-operation (OPRC), 1990
- Protocol on Preparedness, Response and Co-operation to pollution Incidents by Hazardous and Noxious Substances, 2000 (OPRC-HNS Protocol)
- International Convention on the Control of Harmful Anti-fouling Systems on Ships (AFS), 2001
- International Convention for the Control and Management of Ships' Ballast Water and Sediments, 2004
- The Hong Kong International Convention for the Safe and Environmentally Sound Recycling of Ships, 2009

Conventions covering liability and compensation

- International Convention on Civil Liability for Oil Pollution Damage (CLC), 1969
- 1992 Protocol to the International Convention on the Establishment of an International Fund for Compensation for Oil Pollution Damage (FUND 1992)
- Convention relating to Civil Liability in the Field of Maritime Carriage of Nuclear Material(NUCLEAR), 1971
- Athens Convention relating to the Carriage of Passengers and their Luggage by Sea (PAL), 1974
- Convention on Limitation of Liability for Maritime Claims (LLMC), 1976
- International Convention on Liability and Compensation for Damage in Connection with the Carriage of Hazardous and Noxious Substances by Sea (HNS), 1996 (and its 2010 Protocol)
- International Convention on Civil Liability for Bunker Oil Pollution Damage, 2001
- Nairobi International Convention on the Removal of Wrecks, 2007

Other subjects

- International Convention on Tonnage Measurement of Ships (TONNAGE), 1969
- International Convention on Salvage (SALVAGE), 1989

Members of the International Association of Classification Societies (IACS)[18] :

- Indian Register of Shipping (IRS)
- Det Norske Veritas Germanischer Lloyd (DNV GL)
- Lloyd's Register (LR)
- Korean Register of Shipping (KR)
- American Bureau of Shipping (ABS)
- China Classification Society (CCS)
- Nippon Kaiji Kyokai (NK/ClassNK)
- Bureau Veritas (BV)
- Russian Maritime Register of Shipping (RS)
- Registro Italiano Navale (RINA)
- Polish Register of Shipping (PRS)
- Croatian Register of Shipping (CRS)

Subcontracting

The builder may, at its sole discretion and responsibility, subcontract any part of the construction work of the vessel. Usually for minor works the buyer would not interfere, however, for major works the buyer would require the builder to seek his approval which shall not be unreasonably withheld. Major works such as main engine, steering gear system, cargo machinery. To avoid complications, 'Makers list' consisting of a list of subcontractors and suppliers are provided by the builder to the buyer and agreed upon. In *Man B&W Diesel S E Asia Pte and Another v PT Bumi International Tankers and Another Appeal* [2004] 2 SLR(R) 300, the Singapore Court of Appeal clarified the principles governing the recovery of pure economic loss whilst overruling the judgement at first instance. It held that PT Bumi could not sue in tort the engine manufacturer Man B&W for pure economic loss due to defects in the engine as there was no contract between PT Bumi and Man B&W. The defendants did not owe a duty of care. PT Bumi had entered into such contract with the shipbuilder that had limited recourse and the Court attached importance to the limited recourse.

Registration

The ship owner will select the flag that the vessel will fly. The Nationality of a ship is the legal tie between the vessel and her flag state. The flag state is the state where the vessel is registered and therefore becomes entitled to fly her flag. Registration is a process whereby the vessel is entered in the public records of the state. The Classification society (competent authority) issues documentation to a shipowner evidencing vessel's nationality and giving her the right to fly the national flag of that state. In the *Muscat Dhow Case (France v Great Britain)* [19] France was

---

[18] http://www.iacs.org.uk/about/members/
[19] Permanent Court of Arbitration, Muscat Dhows Case, France v Great Britain, The Hague, August 8, 1905
   URL: *http://www.haguejusticeportal.net*

entitled to authorize vessels belonging to the subjects of his Highness the Sultan of Muscat to fly the French flag, only bound by her own legislation and administrative rules. The British protested that the grant of French flags to Arab dhows allowed them to be engage in the slave trade along the East African coast in contravention of the prohibition of slavery adopted by the signatories of the General Act of the Brussels Conference of July 2, 1890.

ARTICLE II – CONTRACT PRICE AND TERMS OF PAYMENT

1. Contract Price:

The purchase price of the VESSEL is ……………………………………………...Japanese Yen (Yen…………………………………………………………………………………………… …………………………..), net receivable by the BUILDER (herein called the "Contract Price"), which is exclusive of the BUYER'S Supplies as provided in Article XVII hereof and shall be subject to upward or downward adjustments, if any, as hereinafter set forth in this Contract.

2. Currency:

Any and all payments by the BUYER to the BUILDER under this Contract shall be made in non-resident convertible free Japanese Yen.

3. Terms of Payment:

The Contract Price shall be paid by the BUYER to the BUILDER in instalments as follows:

(a) 1st Instalment:
The sum of ………………………………………….. Japanese Yen (Yen…………)
shall be paid upon issuance by the Japanese Government of the Export License for the VESSEL.

(b) 2nd Instalment:
The sum of ………………………………………….. Japanese Yen (Yen…………)
shall be paid upon keel-laying of the VESSEL.

(c) 3rd Instalment:
The sum of ………………………………………….. Japanese Yen (Yen…………)
shall be paid upon launching of the VESSEL.

(d) 4th Instalment:
The sum of ………………………………………….. Japanese Yen (Yen…………),
plus any increase or minus any decrease due to adjustments of the Contract Price hereunder, shall be paid upon delivery of the VESSEL.

4. Method of Payment:

(a) 1st Instalment:
Upon receipt of a cable notice from the BUILDER of issuance by the Japanese Government of the Export License for the VESSEL, the BUYER shall remit the amount of this Instalment by telegraphic transfer to The……………………….. Bank Ltd., Tokyo, Japan (herein called "……………………………Bank") for the account of the BUILDER.

(b) 2nd Instalment:

Upon receipt of a cable notice from the BUILDER of keel-laying of the VESSEL having been made, the BUYER shall remit the amount of this Instalment by telegraphic transfer to ……………………. Bank for the account of the BUILDER.

(c) 3rd Instalment:
Upon receipt of a cable notice from the BUILDER of launching of the VESSEL having been made, the BUYER shall remit the amount of this Instalment by telegraphic transfer to ……………………. Bank for the account of the BUILDER.

(d) 4th Instalment:
The BUYER shall, at least seven (7) days prior to the scheduled delivery date of the VESSEL, either cause a prime bank acceptable to the BUILDER through, or to make cash deposit with, …………………………………. Bank, covering the amount of this Instalment as adjusted, available or releasable to the BUILDER against a signed copy of the Protocol of Delivery and Acceptance of the VESSEL as set forth in Paragraph 3 of Article VII hereof.
No payment under this Contract shall be delayed or withheld by the BUYER on account of any dispute or disagreement of whatever nature arising between the parties hereto.

5. Prepayment:

Prepayment of any Instalment due on or before delivery of the VESSEL, shall be subject to mutual agreement between the parties hereto and also subject to approval of the Japanese Government.

ARTICLE II – EXPLANATION

Contract price, currency and terms of payment

The purchase price of the vessel is agreed upon between the builder and the buyer. The price to be paid in the agreed currency. Letter of Intent (LOI) are often said to be more of moral commitment rather than legal. Most shipyards would not like to dispute the LOI for avoiding damage to their reputation. But it must be kept in mind that if the LOI has the elements of a valid contract as explained in Article I such as offer and acceptance, intention to create a legal relationship, consent, competence, consideration, then the LOI will be legally enforceable under English law and Indian law. A point to note that an LOI made fraudulently or negligently will call for an action for damages in tort even if it were not a contract. For example, if a yard states that it will build a gas carrier or oil tanker but does not have the expertise or facility to build a gas carrier or oil tanker.

The famous English case *Adler v Dickson (The Himalaya)* [1954] 3 WLR 696, gave birth to the clause 'Himalaya'. The decision in this case set precedence in contract law. The contract law may permit a contracting party to stipulate exemption from liability for himself as well as third parties whom he engages to perform the contract wholly or partially.

It is usual practice that the payments are done in instalments at certain stages. The 1st instalment will be payable before the construction starts and upon issuance of Export License for the vessel. Some contracts make the first instalment payable once the Builder's Refund Guarantee has been issued to the buyer. Such a refund guarantee secures the buyer's pre-delivery credit risk. If the builder is not able to provide a refund guarantee, then the vessel itself could stand as a security for the buyer's pre-delivery instalments. The 2nd instalment is payable at the laying of the keel. The 3rd instalment is payable upon launching of the vessel. The final 4th instalment is payable upon delivery of the vessel to the buyer. Each party would like to make the contract in their favour. The builder will try to maximise the payments upfront to have least payment due upon delivery, whereas the buyer will try to defer the payments until delivery to minimise the effect of default and the initial capital required. Any default from each side will call for penalties as incorporated in the contract.

In *Stocznia Gdanska S.A.* v. *Latvian Shipping Co., Latreefer Inc. and Others (1998)*[20], there were six shipbuilding contracts, each for the construction of a single refrigerated vessel.

For the "terms of payment", provision was made in clause 5.02 for the price to be paid in four instalments. Broadly speaking these were as follows: (a) five per cent. within seven banking days after receipt by the buyers of a bank guarantee to be furnished by the yard; (b) 20 per cent. within five banking days after the yard had given notice to the buyers of keel laying (defined in the clause as meaning that "the first and second sections of the vessel's hull have been joined on the berth where the vessel is being constructed"); (c) 25 per cent. within five banking days after the yard had given notice to the buyers of the successful launching of the vessel; and (d) the balance of 50 per cent upon delivery of the vessel.

There was another clause 5.05 in the contract, which provided for the rights of the parties following default by the buyers in the payment of any amount due under instalments (b), (c) or (d). Extract from this clause are following:

> "(1) If the purchaser defaults in the payment of any amount due to the seller under sub-clauses (*b*) or (*c*) or (*d*) of clause 5.02 for twenty-one (21) days after the date when such payment has fallen due the seller shall be entitled to rescind the contract. "(2) In the event of such rescission by the seller of this contract due to the purchaser's default as provided for in this clause, the seller shall be entitled to retain and apply the instalments already paid by the purchaser to the recovery of the seller's loss and damage and at the same time the seller shall have the full right and power either to complete or not to complete the vessel and to sell the vessel at a public or private sale on such terms and conditions as the seller deems reasonable provided that the seller is always obliged to mitigate all losses and damages due to any such purchaser's default. "(3) The proceeds received by the seller from the sale and the instalments already paid and retained shall be applied by the seller as mentioned hereinabove as follows: (i) First, in payment of all reasonable costs and expenses of the sale of the vessel. (ii) Second, if the vessel has been completed, in or towards satisfaction of the unpaid balance of the contract price, or if the vessel has not been completed in or towards satisfaction of the unpaid amount of the cost incurred by the seller prior to the date of sale on account of construction of the

---

[20] [1998] 1 All ER 883,
[1998] WLR 574,
[1998] 1 WLR 574,
[1998] UKHL 9
URL: *http://www.bailii.org/uk/cases/UKHL/1998/9.html*

vessel, including work, labour and materials which the seller would have been entitled to receive if the vessel had been completed and delivered. (iii) Third, the balance of the proceeds, if any, shall belong to the purchaser and shall forthwith be paid over to the purchaser by the seller. "(4) In the event of the proceeds from the sale together with payments retained by the seller being insufficient to pay the seller, the purchaser shall be liable for the deficiency and shall pay the same to the seller upon its demand."

Apart from work carried out during laying keels for vessels 1 and 2 nothing else was done for vessels 3, 4, 5 and 6. As per terms of the contract, the first instalments of the price for all six vessels were duly paid.

The keel of vessel 1 was laid, and a keel laying notice was served on the buyers. However, the second instalment for vessel 1 was not paid, and the yard then served on the buyers a notice rescinding the contract under clause 5.05. The same happened with vessel 2. The keel was laid and a keel laying notice was served; but the second instalment for this vessel too was not paid, and again the yard served a notice rescinding the contract under clause 5.05.

The yard sought to take advantage of the keels laid for vessels 1 and 2 in order to trigger the second instalments, first for vessels 3 and 4, and then for vessels 5 and 6. At all events, the keels which had originally been laid in connection with the contracts for vessels 1 and 2 were simply renumbered for vessels 3 and 4, and similarly done for vessels 5 and 6. The second instalments for these vessels were not paid, and the yard gave notice rescinding the contracts for the vessels under clause 5.05. Whether the yard was entitled to act in this way constituted an important issue in the litigation.

In sum, Mr. Justice Thomas held that Latreefers was liable for the repudiation of all six contracts, and liable for damages available at common law on a repudiation basis.[21] The yard claimed that the parent company of the buyers had induced the buyers to breach their contracts with the yard. Thomas J. did find the parent company liable for inducing by unlawful means i.e., failure to provide funds to the buyer to pay the instalments. The Court of Appeal upheld the finding of Thomas J. of the indirect form of tort.

Method of payment of contract price

1st instalment will be due for payment upon receipt of a cable notice from the builder of issuance of the Japanese Government Export License for the vessel, the buyer shall remit the amount by telegraphic transfer to the builder's bank account.

2nd instalment will be due upon receipt of a cable notice from the builder when the vessel keel is laid. The buyer shall remit the amount by telegraphic transfer to the builder's bank account.

3rd instalment will be due upon receipt of a cable notice from the builder when the vessel is launched. The buyer shall remit the amount by telegraphic transfer to the builder's bank account.

---

[21] Stocznia Gdanska SA v Latvian Shipping Co (CA) [2002] 2 Lloyd's Rep. 436.

4th instalment shall be paid by the buyer, at least seven days prior to the scheduled delivery date of the vessel, covering the amount of this instalment as adjusted, available or releasable to the builder against a signed copy of the Protocol of Delivery and Acceptance.

Prepayment

Prepayment of any Instalment due on or before delivery of the vessel, shall be subject to mutual agreement between the parties.

In *Rainy Sky SA and Others v Kookmin Bank*[22], there were six shipbuilding contracts with Jinse Shipbuilding Co Ltd (the builder), a Korean company. The defendant Kookmin Bank issued bonds to the claimants to secure obligations assumed by the builder under the shipbuilding contracts. Each shipbuilding contract entitled the buyer to require the builder to refund the full amount of all advance payments made in the event of the builder's insolvency. A dispute arose as to whether that obligation was covered by the bonds. Each bond was in the form of a letter from the bank to the buyer.

Under the ship building contracts the builder agreed to build and sell one vessel to each of the buyers. The price of each vessel, payable in five equal instalments due at specified points of time, with the final instalment payable on delivery. By an article of the contracts, it was a condition precedent to payment by the buyers of the first instalment that the builder would deliver to the buyers refund guarantees relating to the first and subsequent instalments in a form acceptable to the buyers' financiers. As envisaged by the article, the respondent, Kookmin Bank, issued six materially identical "Advance Payment Bonds", one to each of the buyers.

After the buyers each paid the first instalment due under the contract, the builder experienced financial difficulties and it entered into and/or became subject to a debt workout procedure under the Korean Corporate Restructuring Promotion Law 2007. The buyers wrote to the builder notifying it that this development triggered a particular article of the contract and demanding an immediate refund of all the instalments paid, together with interest at 7 per cent per annum. The builder refused to make any refund on the ground that the particular article of the contracts had not been triggered as alleged. Thus a dispute between the buyers and the builder arose. The buyers wrote to the bank demanding repayment under the bonds of the instalments paid under the contracts. The bank refused to pay. It did so initially on the ground that it was not obliged to pay pending resolution of the dispute between the buyers and the builder.

The issue was whether, on the true construction of the bonds, the buyers are entitled to payment under the bonds in respect of refunds to which they are entitled under the particular article of the contracts. Whether bond covered contractual repayments due from shipbuilder to buyers on insolvency of shipbuilder.

Hoffmann LJ quoted :

---

[22] [2012] 1 Lloyd's Rep. 34.

"But language is a very flexible instrument and, if it is capable of more than one construction, one chooses that which seems most likely to give effect to the commercial purpose of the agreement."

Longmore LJ quoted :

"If a clause is capable of two meanings, it is quite possible that neither meaning will flout common sense, but that, in such a case, it is much more appropriate to adopt the more, rather than the less, commercial construction."

ARTICLE III – ADJUSTMENT OF CONTRACT PRICE

The Contract Price shall be subject to adjustment, as hereinafter set forth, in the event of the following contingencies (it being understood by both parties that any reduction of the Contract Price is by way of liquidated damages and not by way of penalty):

1. Delivery:

(a) No adjustment shall be made and the Contract Price shall remain unchanged for the first thirty (30) days of delay in delivery of the VESSEL beyond the Delivery Date as defined in Article VII hereof (ending as of twelve o'clock midnight of the thirtieth (30th) day of delay).

(b) If the delivery of the VESSEL is delayed more than thirty (30) days after the Delivery Date, then, in such event, beginning at twelve o'clock midnight of the thirtieth (30th) day after the Delivery Date, the Contract Price shall be reduced by deducting therefrom as follows:

31st – 60th day	Yen ……………..	per diem
61st – 90th day	Yen ……………..	per diem
91st – 120th day	Yen ……………..	per diem
121st – 150th day	Yen ……………..	per diem
151st – 180th day	Yen ……………..	per diem
181st – 210th day	Yen ……………..	per diem

However, the total reduction in the Contract Price shall not be more than as would be the case for a delay of hundred and eighty (180) days, counting from midnight of the thirtieth (30th) day after the Delivery Date at the above specified rate of reduction.

(c) But, if the delay in delivery of the VESSEL should continue for a period of hundred and eighty (180) days from the thirty-first (31st) day after the Delivery Date, then in such event, and after such period has expired, the BUYER may at its option rescind this Contract in accordance with the provisions of Article X hereof. The BUILDER may, at any time after the expiration of the aforementioned hundred and eighty (180) days of delay in delivery, if the BUYER has not served notice of rescission as provided in Article X hereof, demand in writing that the BUYER shall make an election, in which case the BUYER shall, within fifteen (15) days after such demand is received by the BUYER, notify the BUILDER of its intention either to rescind this Contract or to consent to the acceptance of the VESSEL at an agreed future date; it being understood by the parties hereto that, if the VESSEL, is not delivered by such future date, the BUYER shall have the same right of rescission upon the same terms and conditions as hereinabove provided.

(d) If the BUYER requests in writing that the delivery of the VESSEL be made earlier than the Delivery Date, and if the delivery of the VESSEL is made, in response to such request of the BUYER, more than thirty (30) days earlier than the Delivery Date, then, in such event, beginning with the thirty-first (31st) day prior to the Delivery Date, the Contract Price of the VESSEL, shall be increased by adding thereto Yen…………………for each full day (it being understood that the BUILDER'S acceptance of such BUYER'S request for early delivery shall be in no way construed as change or alteration of the Delivery Date under this Contract).

19

(e) For the purpose of this Article, the delivery of the VESSEL shall be deemed to be delayed when and if the VESSEL, after taking into full account all postponements of the Delivery Date by reason of permissible delays as defined in Article VIII and/or any other reasons under this Contract, is not delivered by the date upon which delivery is required under the terms of this Contract.

2. Speed:

(a) The Contract Price shall not be affected or changed by reason of the actual speed, as determined by the trial run, being less than three-tenths (3/10) of one (1) knot below the guaranteed speed of the VESSEL.

(b) However, commencing with and including such deficiency of three-tenths (3/10) of one (1) knot in actual speed below the guaranteed speed of the VESSEL, the Contract Price shall be reduced as follows (but disregarding fractions of one-tenth (1/10) of a knot):

For Three-tenths (3/10) of a knot............a total sum of Yen......................

For Four-tenths (4/10) of a knot............a total sum of Yen......................

For Five-tenths (5/10) of a knot............a total sum of Yen......................

For Six-tenths (6/10) of a knot............a total sum of Yen......................

For Seven-tenths (7/10) of a knot............a total sum of Yen......................

For Eight-tenths (8/10) of a knot............a total sum of Yen......................

For Nine-tenths (9/10) of a knot............a total sum of Yen......................

For One (1) knot............................…...........a total sum of Yen......................

(c) If the deficiency in actual speed of the VESSEL upon trial run is more than one (1) full knot below the guaranteed speed of the VESSEL, then the BUYER may, at its option, reject the VESSEL and rescind this Contract in accordance with the provisions of Article X hereof, or may accept the VESSEL at a reduction in the Contract Price as above provided for one (1) full knot only, that is, at a total reduction of Yen..

3. Fuel Consumption:

(a) The Contract Price shall not be affected or changed by reason of the fuel consumption of the VESSEL, as determined by ....trial as per the Specifications, being more than the guaranteed fuel consumption for the VESSEL, if such excess is not more than .... percent (........ %) over the guaranteed fuel consumption.

(b) However, commencing with and including an excess of .... percent (........ %) in the actual fuel consumption over the guaranteed fuel consumption fo the VESSEL, the Contract Price shall be reduced by the sum of Yen... For each full one percent (1%) increase in fuel consumption above said .... percent (............ %) (fractions of one percent (1%) to be prorated), up to a maximum of .... percent (........ %) over the guaranteed fuel consumption of the VESSEL.

(c) If such actual fuel consumption exceeds .... percent (........ %) of the guaranteed fuel consumption of the VESSEL, the BUYER may, at its option, reject the

20

VESSEL and rescind this Contract in accordance with the provisions of Article X hereof, or may accept the VESSEL at a reduction in the Contract Price as above specified for ………….. percent (…….. %) only, that is, at a total reduction of Yen ……………………………………………………………………………..

4. **Deadweight:**

   (a) In the event that the actual deadweight of the VESSEL as determined in accordance with the Specifications is less than or in excess of the guaranteed deadweight of the VESSEL, the Contract Price shall be either reduced by the sum of Yen…………………………….for each full long ton of such deficiency being more than…………………………..(…………………………..) long tons, up to a maximum reduction of Yen…………………………………… , or increased by the sum of Yen…………………………..for each full long ton of such excess being more than…………………………..(…………………………..) long tons, as the case may be (in both cases disregarding fractions of one (1) long ton).

   (b) In the event of such deficiency in the actual deadweight of the VESSEL being…………………………..(…………………………..) long tons or more, then, the BUYER may, at its option, reject the VESSEL and rescind this Contract in accordance with the provisions of Article X hereof or accept the VESSEL at a reduction in the Contract Price as above provided for…………………………..(…………………………..) long tons only, that is, at a total reduction of Yen…………………………………………………………………………………………… …….

5. **Effect of rescission:**

   It is expressly understood and agreed by the parties hereto that in any case, if the BUYER rescinds this Contract under this Article, the BUYER shall not be entitled to any liquidated damages.

ARTICLE III – EXPLANATION

The contract price shall be subject to adjustment, as set forth in the contract, in the event of the certain contingencies. It is understood by both parties that any reduction of the contract price is by way of liquidated damages and not by way of penalty. Section 73 of the Indian Contract Act, 1872 prescribes the damages for loss in case of breach of contract by the defaulting party to the aggrieved party. Liquidated damages are damages which the parties have agreed and fixed as entered into the contract. The damages are explicitly prescribed in the contract where a specific amount is payable in case a party defaults. Let us take a look at the contingencies as mentioned in the SAJ form.

Delivery

As per the SAJ form, there will be no adjustment to the contract price for the first thirty days of delay in delivery of the vessel beyond the delivery date. If the delivery of the vessel is delayed more than thirty days beyond the delivery date, then there will be specified rate of reduction in contract price as given in various periods of thirty days delay such as 31st to 60th day, 61st to 90th day, 91st to 120th day, 121st to 150th day, 151st to 180th day, 181st to 210th day after the delivery date. However, the total reduction in the contract price shall not be more than as would be the case for a delay of hundred and eighty days.

Where the delay takes place beyond the 180 days period from 31 days after the delivery date, the buyer may rescind the contract at its option according to Article X of the form. If the buyer has not served any notice of rescission to the builder, the builder may demand from the buyer in writing to make an election within 15 days whether to rescind the contract or accept the vessel at an agreed future date. The parties will also agree that if there is further delay beyond this agreed future date, then the buyer will have the same right to rescind the contract as per the agreed terms and conditions.

If the buyer requires early delivery of the vessel and the builder delivers the vessel earlier than the delivery date, then, beginning from the thirty first day prior to the delivery date, the contract price of the vessel will be increased at a rate per day as agreed between the parties.

The delay period will start after taking into full account all postponements of the delivery date by reason of permissible delays as defined in Article VIII and any other reason as agreed in the contract.

Speed

As per the SAJ form, there will be no adjustment to the contract price for the speed being less than three-tenths (3/10) of one (1) knot below the guaranteed speed of the vessel. If the speed of the vessel is further less than three-tenths of one knot below the guaranteed speed, then there will be specified rate of reduction in contract price for various speed reductions as three-tenths (3/10) of a knot, four-tenths (4/10) of a knot, five-tenths (5/10) of a knot, six-tenths (6/10) of a knot, seven-tenths (7/10) of a knot, eight-tenths (8/10) of a knot, nine-tenths (9/10) of a knot and for one (1) knot. Where the deficiency in actual speed is more than one (1) knot, then the buyer may reject the vessel and rescind the contract or accept the vessel at the agreed reduction in contract price for one (1) knot.

Fuel Consumption

As per the SAJ form, the buyer and builder will agree to an acceptable percentage of fuel consumption more than the guaranteed fuel consumption for the vessel for which there will be no adjustment to the contract price. For fuel consumption in excess of such agreed percentage, there will be reduction to the contract price for each one (1) percent increase at the agreed rate upto a certain maximum fuel consumption percentage. Thereafter, any further increase in consumption percentage to the maximum allowed, the buyer may reject the vessel and rescind the contract or accept the vessel at the maximum consumption percentage agreed reduction in contract price.

Deadweight

As per the SAJ form, the contract price will be reduced if the actual deadweight capacity is less than the guaranteed deadweight capacity and the contract price will be increased if the actual deadweight capacity is more than the guaranteed. The reduction or increase in the contract price will be agreed at a particular price per long ton change in the deadweight capacity. At an agreed maximum tolerance, the buyer may reject the vessel and rescind the contract or accept the vessel at a reduction in the contract price.

Effect of rescission

As per the SAJ form, the buyer and builder agree that if the buyer rescinds the contract then the buyer shall not be entitled to any liquidated damages.

In *K/S A/S Bani and K/S A/S Havbulk I v. Korea Shipbuilding and Engineering Corporation*[23], by two shipbuilding contracts made in July 1983 between the builders and the buyers, the builders undertook to construct equip and complete two Probo carriers each of 37,000 tonnes deadweight. The vessels were to be built in accordance with the contract specification and a general arrangement plan. Construction was to be in accordance with the rules of the Det Norske Veritas and the price of each vessel was agreed. Twelve percent of this sum was to be paid at various stages before and during construction and a fifth instalment of 8 percent was to be paid on delivery. The balance was to be paid over eight years following delivery by promissory notes secured by banker's guarantee or letter of credit.

The due date for delivery was August, 1985. The builders asserted that the sea trials had been duly completed on February 11, 1986 and gave notice that they intended to deliver the vessels on February 25. The buyers gave notice of rejection on February 14 alleging that the vessels did not conform. The builders disputed the buyers right to reject the vessel and tendered delivery. The buyers refused to accept delivery, to pay the fifth instalments of the price and to furnish promissory notes and guarantees. The buyers cancelled the contracts.

---

[23] [1987] 2 Lloyd's Rep. 445.

ARTICLE IV – APPROVAL OF PLANS AND DRAWINGS AND INSPECTION DURING CONSTRUCTION

1. Approval of Plans and Drawings:

(a) The BUILDER shall submit to the BUYER three (3) copies each of the plans and drawings to be submitted thereto for its approval at its address as set forth in Article XVIII hereof. The BUYER shall, within fourteen (14) days after receipt thereof, return to the BUILDER one (1) copy of such plans and drawings with the BUYER'S approval or comments written thereon, if any. A list of the plans and drawings to be so submitted to the BUYER shall be mutually agreed upon between the parties hereto.

(b) When and if the Representative shall have been sent by the BUYER to the Shipyard in accordance with Paragraph 2 of this Article, the BUILDER may submit the remainder, if any, of the plans and drawings in the agreed list, to the Representative for its approval, unless otherwise agreed upon between the parties hereto. The Representative shall, within seven (7) days after receipt thereof, return to the BUILDER one (1) copy of such plans and drawings with his approval or comments written thereon, if any. Approval by the Representative of the plans and drawings duly submitted to him shall be deemed to be the approval by the BUYER for all purposes of the Contract.

(c) In the event that the BUYER or the Representative shall fail to return the plans and drawings to the BUILDER within the time limit as hereinabove provided, such plans and drawings shall be deemed to have been automatically approved without any comment.

2. Appointment of BUYER'S Representative:

The BUYER may send to and maintain at the Shipyard, at the BUYER'S own cost and expense, one representative who shall be duly authorized in writing by the BUYER (herein called the "Representative") to act on behalf of the BUYER in connection with modifications of the Specifications, adjustments of the Contract Price, approval of the plans and drawings, attendance to the tests and inspections relating to the VESSEL, its machinery, equipment and outfitting, and any other matters for which he is specifically authorized by the BUYER.

3. Inspection by Representative:

The necessary inspections of the VESSEL, its machinery, equipment and outfittings shall be carried out by the Classification Society, other regulatory bodies and/or an inspection team of the BUILDER throughout the entire period of construction, in order to ensure that the construction of the VESSEL is duly performed in accordance with this Contract and the Specifications. The Representative shall have, during construction of the VESSEL, the right to attend such tests and inspections of the VESSEL, its machinery and equipment as are mutually agreed between the BUYER and BUILDER. The BUILDER shall give a notice to the Representative reasonably in advance of the date and place of such tests and inspections to be attended by him for his convenience.

Failure of the Representative to be present at such tests and inspections after due notice to him as above provided shall be deemed to be a waiver of his right to be present.

In the event that the Representative discovers any construction or material or workmanship which is not deemed to conform to the requirements of this Contract and/or Specifications, the representative shall promptly give the BUILDER a notice in writing as to such non-conformity. Upon receipt of such notice from the Representative, the BUILDER shall correct such non-conformity, if the BUILDER agrees to his view. In all working hours during the construction of the VESSEL until delivery thereof, the Representative shall be given free and ready access to the VESSEL , its engines and accessories, and to any other place where work is being done, or materials are being processed or stored, in connection with the construction of the VESSEL, including the yards, workshops, stores and offices of the BUILDER, and the premises of subcontractors of the BUILDER, who are doing work or storing materials in connection with the VESSEL'S construction.

4. Facilities:

The BUILDER shall furnish the Representative and his assistant(s) with adequate office space, and such other reasonable facilities according to the BUILDER'S practice at or in the immediate vicinity of the Shipyard as may be necessary to enable them to effectively carry out their duties.

5. Liabilities of the BUILDER:

The Representative and his assistant(s) shall at all times be deemed to be the employees of the BUYER and not of the BUILDER. The BUILDER shall be under no liability whatsoever to the BUYER, the Representative or his assistant(s) for personal injuries, including death, suffered during the time when he or they are on the VESSEL, or within the premises of either the BUILDER or its subcontractors, or are otherwise engaged in and about the construction of the VESSEL, unless, however, such personal injuries, including death, were caused by a gross negligence of the BUILDER, or of any of its employees or agents or subcontractors. Nor shall the BUILDER be under any liability whatsoever to the BUYER, the Representative or his assistant(s) for damage to, or loss or destruction of property in Japan of the BUYER or of the Representative or his assistant(s), unless such damage, loss or destruction were caused by a gross negligence of the BUILDER, or of any of its employees or agents or subcontractors.

6. Responsibility of BUYER:

The BUYER shall undertake and assure that the Representative shall carry out his duties hereunder in accordance with the normal shipbuilding practice of the BUILDER and in such a way as to avoid any unnecessary increase in building cost, delay in the construction of the VESSEL, and/or any disturbance in the construction schedule of the BUILDER.

The BUILDER has the right to request the BUYER to replace the Representative who is deemed unsuitable and unsatisfactory for the proper progress of the VESSEL'S construction. The BUYER shall investigate the situation by sending its representative(s) to the Shipyard if necessary, and if the BUYER considers that such BUILDER'S request is justified, the BUYER shall effect such replacement as soon as conveniently arrangeable.

ARTICLE IV – EXPLANATION

Plans and drawings are one of the most important integral part of the ship building contract. The buyer aspires to buy a particular type of ship suitable for a particular trade and trading area. Accordingly, the ship will be constructed by the builder. Any building needs a plan and drawings and ship building is no exception. The important thing is that such plans and drawings needs to be approved by the classification society and the regulatory authorities. The buyer and builder, usually through their representatives, will sit down and negotiate what is required and what is not whilst taking into consideration the latest rules and regulations governing such type of vessel. The other crucial factor will be the given time frame to complete the project and the cost involved. The builder is ultimately responsible for the vessel's design and will be held liable for any deficiency. It is prudent for the buyer that such intent is expressed in the contract so that the builder does not escape his liability for the vessel's design defect. The contractual language should clearly cite that the approval of the plans and drawings by the buyer does not alter the builder's responsibility for the vessel's design. This would then prevent the operation of an estoppel defence.

It is usual practice, that during the course of the construction of the vessel, the buyer and builder technical teams work closely alongwith the classification society to ensure that the vessel plans and drawings are approved and thereby avoid delays to the building time frame. In order to avoid delays in approval by the buyer, the SAJ form incorporates time frames within which period the buyer must approve the plans and drawings.

Approval of Plans and Drawings

As per the SAJ form, the builder submits three copies of plans and drawings to the buyer for its approval. The buyer must return one copy of the plans and drawings to the builder with approval or comments, if any, within a period of fourteen days. Such plans and drawings to be submitted to the buyer must be mutually agreed between the parties. If the buyer has representative in the shipyard, the builder may submit any remaining plans and drawings of the agreed list to the representative for its approval. In such case, the representative must return one copy of the plans and drawings to the builder with approval or comments, if any, within a period of seven days. The approval by the representative will be deemed to be the approval by the buyer for the purposes of the contract. If the buyer or the representative fail to return the plans and drawings within the time limit, then such plans and drawings shall be deemed to have been approved automatically without any comment.

Appointment of Buyer's Representative

The buyer may appoint a representative at the shipyard at its own cost and expense. Such appointment should be duly notified to the builder. The representative will be duly authorized by the buyer in writing to act on its behalf. The representative can modify the specifications, adjust the contract price, approve plans and drawings, be present at the time of sea trials, tests and inspections relating to the vessel, its machinery, equipment and outfitting for which he is authorized by the buyer. The scope of the representative's work will be clearly identified by the buyer.

Inspection by Buyer's Representative

The buyer's representative at the shipyard shall have the right to attend the tests and inspections of the vessel, its machinery and equipment as and when it is carried out by the classification society, other regulatory bodies or an inspection team of the builder. Usually an office is allocated to the representative within the shipyard or in the vicinity. The office should have facilities as may be necessary to enable representative and his assistants to effectively carry out their duties. An example of the facilities would be adequate office space with working desks, chairs, computers, printers, photocopy machine, fax, internet access, cupboards, changing lockers, bathrooms, pantry.

The representative is given free and ready access to the vessel during the working hours and as permitted by the shipyard in the course of the construction of the vessel, including the yards, workshops, stores and offices of the builder and the premises of the subcontractors of the builder who are involved in the construction of the vessel.

The representative must be given reasonable advance notice by the builder of such tests and inspections including the date and place where it will be conducted. If the representative fails to attend such tests and inspections after due notice to him by the builder, then it shall be deemed to be a waiver of his right to be present.

If the representative finds any defect in the construction or material or workmanship which is not in accordance to the contract or specifications, then he must promptly give a notice in writing to the builder of such non-conformity. The builder shall correct this defect if agreed.

Liabilities of the Builder

The builder is not liable to the buyer for the acts or omission of the buyer's representative and his assistants as they are the employees of the buyer. The builder cannot be held responsible for the personal injuries or death suffered by the representative or his assistants on the vessel or in the builder's premises or the builder's subcontractor's premises unless it is caused due to gross negligence of the builder or its subcontractors. Similarly, the builder cannot be held liable for damage or loss or destruction of property of the BUYER or of the Representative or his assistants, unless such damage, loss or destruction were caused by a gross negligence of the builder or its subcontractors.

Responsibility of Buyer

The main reason of having a representative on site is for the buyer to have his presence in the shipyard during the course of construction of the vessel. To safeguard his interest and have a day to day inspection of the vessel and keep the buyer updated of the construction progress and any issues whatsoever. Whilst carrying out its duties, the representative shall carry out his duties in accordance with the normal shipbuilding practice of the builder and avoid any unnecessary increase in building cost, delay in the construction of the vessel or cause any disturbance in the construction schedule of the builder. The representative must avoid needless arguments, meetings, which would further effect the delivery date of the vessel unless it is absolutely necessary and reasonable. If the representative is deemed unsuitable and unsatisfactory for the purpose, the builder has a right to request the buyer to replace the representative. If, after due investigation, the buyer considers that the builder's request is justified, then the buyer shall replace the representative. This is rare because most of the representatives are experts in ship construction. They have sound knowledge of the construction of the vessel and are well versed with the shipbuilding practice of the builder.

ARTICLE V – MODIFICATIONS

1. Modifications of Specifications :

The Specifications may be modified and/or changed by written agreement of the parties thereto, provided that such modifications and/or changes or an accumulation thereof will not, in the BUILDER'S judgement, adversely affect the BUILDER'S planning or program in relation to the BUILDER'S other commitments, and provided, further, that the BUYER shall first agree, before such modifications and/or changes are carried out, to alterations in the Contract Price, the Delivery Date and other terms and conditions of this Contract and Specifications occasioned by or resulting from such modifications and/or changes.
Such agreement may be effected by exchange of letters signed by the authorized representatives of the parties hereto or by cables confirmed by such letters manifesting agreements of the parties hereto which shall constitute amendments to this Contract and/or the Specifications.
The BUILDER may make minor changes to the Specifications, if found necessary for introduction of improved production methods or otherwise, provided that the BUILDER shall first obtain the BUYER'S approval which shall not be unreasonably withheld.

2. Change in Class, etc.:

In the event that, after the date of this Contract, any requirements as to class, or as to rules and regulations to which the construction of the VESSEL is required to conform are altered or changed by the Classification Society or the other regulatory bodies authorized to make such alterations or changes, the following provisions shall apply:

(a) If such alterations or changes are compulsory for the VESSEL, either of the parties hereto, upon receipt of such information from the Classification Society or such other regulatory bodies, shall promptly transmit the same to the other in writing, and the BUILDER shall thereupon incorporate such alterations or changes into the construction of the VESSEL, provided that the BUYER shall first agree to adjustments required by the BUILDER in the Contract Price, the Delivery Date and other terms and conditions of this Contract and the Specifications occasioned by or resulting from alterations or changes.

(b) If such alterations or changes are not compulsory for the VESSEL, but the BUYER desires to incorporate such alterations or changes into the construction of the VESSEL, then, the BUYER shall notify the BUILDER of such intention. The BUILDER may accept such alterations or changes, provided that such alterations or changes will not, in the judgement of the BUILDER, adversely affect the BUILDER'S planning or program in relation to the BUILDER'S other commitments, and provided , further, that the BUYER shall first agree to adjustments required by the BUILDER in the Contract Price, the Delivery Date and other terms and conditions of this Contract and the Specifications occasioned by or resulting from such alterations or changes.

Agreements as to such alterations or changes under this Paragraph shall be made in the same manner as provided in Paragraph 1 of this article for modifications or changes to the Specifications.

3. **Substitution of Materials:**

In the event that any of the materials required by the Specifications or otherwise under this Contract for the constructions of the VESSEL cannot be procured in time or are in short supply to maintain the Delivery Date of the VESSEL, the BUILDER may, provided that the BUYER shall so agree in writing, supply other materials capable of meeting the requirements of the Classification Society and of the rules, regulations and requirements with which the construction of the VESSEL must comply. Any agreement as to such substitution of materials shall be effected in the manner provided in Paragraph 1 of this Article, and shall, likewise, include alterations in the Contract Price and other terms and conditions of this Contract occasioned by or resulting from such substitution.

ARTICLE V – EXPLANATION

It is quite normal during ship building to have modifications to the vessel. This could be due to various reasons. It could be that that buyer wants the modifications so as to fulfill changes in his plans. It also could be due to change in regulations of classification society or regulatory authorities. For example, when the International Maritime Organization (IMO), through its Marine Environment Protection Committee (MEPC), introduced regulations for the prevention of air pollution under Annex VI of the MARPOL Convention[24], several ships were modified to accommodate the NOx requirements.

Modifications of Specifications

As per the SAJ form, the buyer and builder may modify the specifications by written agreement. When the buyer seeks such modifications, it should not affect the builder's schedule or other commitments. Also the buyer shall agree to the resultant changes in the contract price, delivery date and to other terms and conditions of the contract which are effected due to such modifications.

Similarly, if the builder seeks to modify the specifications, he must first obtain the buyer's approval. The buyer should not hold back the approval unreasonably.

When doing any modification, sufficient documentation, particulars and details of the modification must be provided so as to estimate the time required to carry out such modification and the cost involved. The builder must ensure to minimize the cost of such

---

[24] International Convention on the Prevention of Pollution from Ships, 1973 as modified by the Protocols of 1978 and 1997 (MARPOL 73/78).

modification and it should not have negative impact on the vessel's proposed capacity and performance.

Change in Class, etc.

Where new regulations come into force after the contract has been entered, inorder to comply with such regulations, the vessel will be required to be modified accordingly. When either of the parties are aware of such regulation coming into force, then the same must be promptly brought to the notice of the other party in writing. The builder shall incorporate such alterations and modifications to the vessel provided that the buyer first agrees to the adjustment in the contract price, any changes to the delivery date and changes to the other terms and conditions of the contract. When such changes are not compulsory for the vessel and modification is not required, but the buyer insists on having the modification done, then the buyer must make his intention clear to the builder. Buyer must inform the builder in writing of his intention. If the said proposal of the buyer does not affect the builder's schedule or his other commitments, then the builder may accept such changes or modifications. Prior doing the modifications, the buyer must first agree to the resultant changes in the contract price, delivery date and to other terms and conditions of the contract which are effected due to such modifications.

Substitution of Materials

When any material that is required by specifications for the construction of the vessel under the contract is not available due to short supply or such materials cannot be delivered in time so as to maintain the delivery date of the vessel, the builder may substitute such materials with other suitable materials provided it is approved by the buyer in writing. Such substituted materials must meet the requirements of the classification society and of the regulatory authorities with which the construction of the vessel must comply. Prior doing the modifications, the buyer must first agree to the resultant changes in the contract price, delivery date and to other terms and conditions of the contract which are effected due to such modifications.

ARTICLE VI – TRIALS

1. Notice :

The BUYER shall receive from the BUILDER at least fourteen (14) days prior notice in writing or by cable confirmed in writing of the time and place of the trial run for the VESSEL, and the BUYER shall promptly acknowledge receipt of such notice. The BUYER shall have its representative on board the VESSEL to witness such trial run. Failure in attendance of the representative of the BUYER at the trial run of the VESSEL for any reason whatsoever after due notice to the BUYER as above provided shall be deemed to be a waiver by the BUYER of its right to have its representative on board the VESSEL at the trial run, and the BUILDER may conduct the trial run without the representative of the BUYER being present, and in such case the BUYER shall be obligated to accept the VESSEL on the basis of a certificate of the BUILDER that the VESSEL, upon trial run, is found to conform to this Contract and the Specifications.

2. Weather Condition :

The trial run shall be carried out under the weather condition which is deemed favourable enough by the judgement of the BUILDER. In the event of unfavourable weather on the date specified for the trial run, the same shall take place on the first available day thereafter that the weather condition permits. It is agreed that, if during the trial run of the VESSEL, the weather should suddenly become so unfavourable that orderly conduct of the trial run can no longer be continued, the trial run shall be discontinued and postponed until the first favourable day next following, unless the BUYER shall assent in writing to acceptance of the VESSEL on the basis of the trial run already made before such discontinuance has occurred. Any delay of trial run caused by such unfavourable weather condition shall operate to postpone the Delivery Date by the period of delay involved and such delay shall be deemed as a permissible delay in the delivery of the VESSEL.

3. How Conducted :

(a) All expenses in connection with the trial run are to be for the account of the BUILDER and the BUILDER shall provide at its own expense the necessary crew to comply with conditions of safe navigation. The trial run shall be conducted in the manner prescribed in the Specifications, and shall prove fulfilment of the performance requirements of the trial run as set forth in the Specifications. The course of trial run shall be determined by the BUILDER.

(b) Notwithstanding the foregoing, fuel oil lubricating oil and greases necessary for the trial run of the VESSEL shall be supplied by the BUYER at the Shipyard prior to the time of the trial run, and the BUILDER shall pay the BUYER upon delivery of the VESSEL the cost of the quantities of fuel oil, lubricating oil and greases consumed during the trial run at the original purchase price. In measuring the consumed quantity, lubricating oils and greases remaining in the main engine, other machinery and their pipes, stern tube and the like, shall be excluded. The quantity of fuel oil, lubricating oils and greases supplied by the BUYER shall be in accordance with the instruction of the BUILDER.

4. **Method of Acceptance or Rejection :**

(a) Upon completion of the trial run, the BUILDER shall give the BUYER a notice by cable confirmed in writing of completion of the trial run, as and if the BUILDER considers that the results of the trial run indicate conformity of the VESSEL to this Contract and the Specifications. The BUYER shall, within three (3) days after receipt of such notice from the BUILDER, notify the BUILDER by cable confirmed in writing of its acceptance or rejection of the VESSEL.

(b) However, should the results of the trial run indicate that the VESSEL, or any part or equipment thereof, does not conform to the requirements of this Contract and /or the Specifications, or if the BUILDER is in agreement to non-conformity as specified in the BUYER'S notice of rejection, then the BUILDER shall take necessary steps to correct such non-conformity. Upon completion of correction of such non-conformity, the BUILDER shall give the BUYER a notice thereof by cable confirmed in writing. The BUYER shall, within two (2) days after receipt of such notice from the BUILDER, notify the BUILDER of its acceptance or rejection of the VESSEL.

(c) In any event that the BUYER rejects the VESSEL, the BUYER shall indicate in its notice of rejection in what respect the VESSEL, or any part or equipment thereof does not conform to this Contract and /or the Specifications.

(d) In event that the BUYER fails to notify the BUILDER by cable confirmed in writing of the acceptance of or the rejection together with the reason therefore of the VESSEL within the period as provided in the above Sub-paragraph (a) or (b), the BUYER shall be deemed to have accepted the VESSEL.

The BUILDER may dispute the rejection of the VESSEL by the BUYER under this Paragraph, in which case the matter shall be submitted for final decision by arbitration in accordance with Article XIII hereof.

5. **Effect of Acceptance :**

Acceptance of the VESSEL as above provided shall be final and binding so far as conformity of the VESSEL to this Contract and the Specifications is concerned and shall preclude the BUYER from refusing formal delivery of the VESSEL as hereinafter provided, if the BUILDER complies with all other procedural requirements for delivery as provided in Article VII hereof.

6. **Disposition of Surplus Consumable Stores :**

Should any fresh water or other consumable stores furnished by the BUILDER for the trial run remain on board the VESSEL at the time of acceptance thereof by the BUYER, the BUYER agrees to buy the same from the BUILDER at the original purchase price thereof,

and payment by the BUYER shall be
effected upon delivery of the VESSEL.

ARTICLE VI – EXPLANATION

This is a major step towards completion of the ship construction. All the hard work that has been put by thousands of workers which include but not limited to Naval architects, engineers, welders, electricians, designers, electronic and computer technicians will now be seen to the fore during the vessel trials. Once all the construction and outfitting work has been completed, the trials will be conducted by the shipyard in the presence of the classification society, regulatory authority, buyers representatives. At this time, the buyer representatives may include senior officers of the ships crew who are present in the shipyard in order to take the delivery of the vessel.

Notice

As per SAJ form, the builder must give at least fourteen days notice to the buyer in writing stating the date, time and place of the trial run for the vessel. The buyer must promptly acknowledge this notice of the builder. The buyer shall place his representatives onboard to witness the trial run of the vessel. If the buyer fails to place his representatives onboard to witness the trial run after having acknowledged the notice of the builder, it shall be deemed that the buyer has waived his rights to witness the trial run of the vessel. The builder will then go ahead and conduct the trial run of the vessel without the buyers representatives and in such case the buyer will have to accept the vessel on the basis of a certificate from the builder stating that the vessel complies with the contract and the specifications. This usually does not happen, but it is incorporated into the contract so as to be in favour of the builder in case of buyer missing the deadline of placing his representatives onboard the vessel for the trial run.

Weather Condition

The SAJ form provides for the trial run to be conducted in weather conditions which is deemed favourable as per the judgement of the builder. Hence it is the builder who will decide when and where the trials are going to be conducted. Typically, the weather conditions favourable for the trial run are wind speed 10 knots or less and calm seas. The area where the trials are conducted are generally near the shipyard within the territorial waters of the country. In case the weather conditions are worse, unfavourable to carry out the trial run, then the same shall be conducted at the next available day when the weather conditions are favourable. Any delay such caused shall result in the postponement of the delivery date by the period of delay and such delay shall be deemed as a permissible delay in the delivery of the vessel.

How Conducted

As per the SAJ form, the trial run will be carried out by the builder at his expense and the course of the trial run will be determined by the builder. It is obvious that since the title has not been passed to the buyer, the risk remains with the builder. The crew required for safe navigation of the vessel will be provided by the builder. Any crew who are placed onboard by the buyer after seeking permission from the builder are mere observers and should not interfere with the trial run. The trial run will be carried out pursuant to the specifications and the aim will be to prove fulfilment of the performance requirements as set forth in the specifications.

According to the SAJ form, the fuel oil, lubricating oil and greases that are required for the trial run of the vessel shall be supplied by the buyer as per the instructions of the builder. The quantity of fuel oil, lubricating oil and grease that will be consumed during the trial run will be on builders account. The builder shall pay the cost of the consumption to the buyer.

Method of Acceptance or Rejection

Once the trial run of the vessel has been completed then the question arises whether the vessel satisfied the performance expected as per the contract and specifications. Shipbuilding is complex involving several machinery and equipments and it is normal that there would be several defects that would be observed and would need to be rectified. As per the SAJ form, the builder gives the buyer three days notice in writing of the vessel having completed the trial run and that the trial run was successful which indicates that the vessel conforms to the contract and the specifications. The buyer after receiving the notice from the builder shall reply in writing within three days, confirming to the builder whether he accepts or rejects the vessel.

If the vessel trial run performance does not conform to the contract and the specifications and the builder accepts the non-conformity notice of rejection of the buyer, then the builder shall rectify the defects of non-conformity. The buyer provides a list of defects that needs to be rectified by the builder. As soon as the defects are rectified, the builder shall give two days notice in writing to the buyer stating the completion of correction of such non-conformity. The buyer after receiving such notice, within a period of two days notify the builder whether he accepts or rejects the vessel. In case the buyer rejects the vessel, then the buyer must inform the buyer as to why he is rejecting the vessel. The buyer must inform in what respect the vessel does not conform to the contract and the specifications. If the buyer after receiving the builder's notice fails to confirm in writing to the builder within a period of two days whether the buyer accepts or rejects the vessel, then the buyer shall be deemed to have accepted the vessel. Wherein a dispute arises between the builder and the buyer subject to rejection of the vessel by the buyer, then the matter will be decided by arbitration in accordance with Article XII of the SAJ form.

Effect of Acceptance

Once the buyer has accepted the vessel after the trial run of the vessel and due procedure followed as was explained above, then the acceptance shall be deemed final and binding so far as conforming to the contract and the specifications. It will preclude the buyer from refusing formal delivery of the vessel provided that the builder complies with all other procedural requirements for delivery as provided in Article VII of the SAJ form.

Disposition of Surplus Consumable Stores :

As per the SAJ form, after the trial run has been completed and if there are any surplus consumable stores that have been provided by the builder for the trial run which remain onboard the vessel at the time of acceptance of the vessel by the buyer, then the buyer agrees to pay the builder the original purchase price of the surplus consumables upon delivery of the vessel.

A guide to procedure for the sea trial

1. Normally there would be a check list prior to the sea trial which is completed and this is confirmed by Builder's confirmation.

2. The sea trial is conducted when the wind and sea state are less than or equal to Beaufort force 3.

3. The Class notation would be included.

4. The Loadicator also known as the Loading computer is used to assess the stability conditions of the vessel. This must be commissioned and ready for use before the sea trial.

5. Before the sea trial is carried out, the visual draughts are checked and the actual displacement is calculated. The density of the seawater is also measured. The vessel displacement is measured using the hull trimmed hydrostatic tables which must be available on board. The loadicator is used to cross check the vessel condition such as the displacement, IMO stability requirements of intact stability, trim, list, Longitudinal strength, shearing forces, bending moments, torsional stress, etc.

6. The shearing force and bending moment diagram must be included for the sea trial condition.

7. The displacement and trim for sea trial condition should be the same as per model test condition. The model test draught, displacement, trim condition should be included in the sea trial procedure for reference.

8. All Calibration instruments are to be available onboard.

9. ISO 15016:2015 standard to be used for evaluation of the speed and the Energy Efficiency Design Index (EEDI) calculation. The EEDI for new ships is the single most important technical measure aimed at promoting the use of more energy efficient equipment and engines. The EEDI provides a specific figure for an individual ship design, expressed in grams of carbon dioxide (CO_2) per ship's capacity-mile. The smaller the EEDI, the more energy efficient is the ship's design and it is a simple formula that estimates CO_2 output per tonne-mile.

10. The vibration measurement is carried out using special equipment which are noise and vibration machine sensors. The sensors are calibrated before the sea trial. The measurement of vibration response of hull girder and accommodation space procedure is to be provided. The purpose of the measurement is to find out the vibration level and to investigate the dynamic characteristics of the vessel. Transducer for hull girder vibration and for Main Engine shaft is provided for recording vertical, longitudinal and transversal vibrations. Where the noise or vibration level exceed the limits provided by relative standards, a corrective action has to be taken by the shipyard upon mutual agreement with the buyer. Additional vibration check points can be put in following locations on the vessel but not limited to:

a) Main mast and associated platforms on monkey island, over wheel house
b) Navigation Bridge wings
c) Engine casing (from bottom up to the funnel top)
d) Two points on each engine room deck
e) Provision crane pedestal
f) Two points on main deck
g) Midship crane pedestal
h) Mast risers
i) Diesel Generator bed plate #1, 2 & 3
j) Boiler platform
k) Main Air Compressor

11. Fire fighting system as following but not limited to:

l) Fire detection and alarm system test
m) Hyper mist system
n) CO2 fire fighting system
o) Deck water spray for fire fighting system to be demonstrated
p) All portable extinguishers to be checked prior installation, usually it is buyers option but may be provided by the builder if agreed by the buyer.
q) Main fire pump and emergency fire pump alongwith the fire lines on deck, engine room and accommodation.

12. Various equipments to be demonstrated to the ship's crew as per the agreement between the builder and buyer. A list to be provided before sea trial as to the arrangement of various service engineers.

13. The equipments on the wheel house for the navigation of the ship are to be checked and adjusted.

14. The Echo sounder to be checked. This is used for measuring the depth of water.

Main Engine related

15. All the safety devices of the Main Engine are to be checked before starting the Main Engine.

16. The shipyard shaft torsion meter must be calibrated in the presence of buyer representatives before commencement of the test. The shaft torsion meter is used for measuring the power of the main engine.

17. During speed trial, specific fuel consumption is measured at each run (for example 50, 75, 90 and100 percent load on the Main Engine) for the buyer's information and records.

18. Main Engine Jack-up and deflection (Hot Condition) is carried out. The intermediate shaft bearing reaction force check including Main Engine last three bearings is carried out in hot

condition before de-ballasting.

19. Main Engine holding down bolts are to be re-tightened after the sea trial.

20. Fuel changeover procedure is to be demonstrated as per approved fuel changeover procedure. This is to comply with the MARPOL Annex VI and areas with stringent requirement also called the Emission Control Areas (ECA). The changeover is mainly from the high sulphur fuel oil to low sulphur fuel oil in ECA. The SOx emission is purely dependent on the quality of the fuel oil and the sulphur content therein.

21. Progressive speed trial is carried out. The test is carried out with different engine loads in order to settle relation between ship's speed and engine load (for example 50, 75, 90 and 100 percent load on the Main Engine). The speed trial results are corrected to calm condition (no wind, no wave), no current and deep sea condition according to ISO 15016:2015 trial analysis method. All the observations are to be recorded under condition that ship's speed and shaft revolution are steady. The approach run must be of sufficient distance to obtain steady condition.

22. Engine room machinery test. This mainly involves the Main Engine starting test, Main Engine minimum revolution test, bridge control test, endurance test (Main Engine load & Speed at M.C.R. for 2 hours & N.C.R. for 4 hours), dead ship recovery test, Exhaust gas boiler test, fresh water generator running test, steering gear test, emergency steering gear test, torsional vibration test, black out and recovery test.

23. Manoeuvring tests[25]:

   a) The purpose of the Turning trial is to know the following:

      1. Ship's turning manoeuvrability - Turning circle manoeuvre is the manoeuvre to be performed to both starboard and port with 35° rudder angle or the maximum rudder angle permissible at the test speed, following a steady approach with zero yaw rate.,

      2. Advance - Advance is the distance travelled in the direction of the original course by the midship point of a ship from the position at which the rudder order is given to the position at which the heading has changed 90° from the original course.

      3. Transfer - Transfer is the distance travelled by the midship point of a ship from the position at which the rudder order is given to the position at which the heading has changed 90° from the original course. It is measured in a direction perpendicular to the original heading of the ship.

      4. Tactical diameter - Tactical diameter is the distance travelled by the midship point of a ship from the position at which the rudder order is given to the position at which the heading has changed 180° from the original course. It is measured in a direction perpendicular to the original heading of the ship.

[25] http://www.imo.org/en/KnowledgeCentre/IndexofIMOResolutions/Maritime-Safety-Committee-(MSC)/Documents/MSC.137(76).pdf.

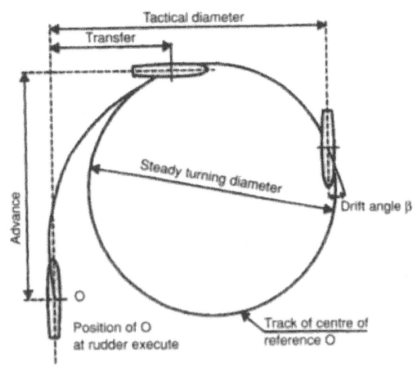

b) Zig-zag trial - The purpose of zig-zag trial is to know the ship's course stability and how the ship responds to changes in the rudder angle. Zig-zag test is the manoeuvre where a known amount of helm is applied alternately to either side when a known heading deviation from the original heading is reached.

c) Crash stop astern and ahead trial - The purpose of the crash stop astern trial is to prove that the Main Engine is suitable to ship's emergency stop and to know the time and sailing distance between order of astern under headway and ship's stop. It is the distance travelled from the astern order point to the ship stop point.

The yard compiles and supplies a "Manoeuvring Booklet" in accordance with IMO Resolution 137(76) to the vessel and buyer.

24. Life Boat, Rescue Boat launching test. The test shall be carried out to demonstrate that the life boat and rescue boat complies with the SOLAS and it can be launched from the ship proceeding ahead at a speed of not less than 5 knots in calm water. This test is usually done at the end of the sea trial when the ship is returning back to the ship yard.

25. The Anchor windlass test procedure is to be carried out to prove the windlass performance. This involves letting go of the anchors to reach the seabed at an appropriate depth taking into account the prevailing conditions and holding the brakes tight. The hoisting and lowering speed of the anchor chain is recorded.

26. The ship is swung in open sea and the magnetic compass is adjusted by compass adjuster. The deviation curve table is made for the vessel.

27. The result of sea trial booklet is prepared and submitted to the buyer for approval.

ARTICLE VII – DELIVERY

1. Time and Place :

The VESSEL shall be delivered by the BUILDER to the BUYER at the Shipyard on or before..................., 19..................., except that, in the event of delays in the construction of the VESSEL or any performance required under this Contract due to causes which under the terms of this Contract permit postponement of the date for delivery, the aforementioned date for delivery of the VESSEL shall be postponed accordingly. The aforementioned date, or such later date to which the requirement of delivery is postponed pursuant to such terms, is herein called the "Delivery Date".

2. When and How Effected :

Provided that the BUYER shall have fulfilled all of its obligations stipulated under this Contract, delivery of the VESSEL shall be effected forthwith by the concurrent delivery by each of the parties hereto to the other of the PROTOCOL OF DELIVERY AND ACCEPTANCE, acknowledging delivery of the VESSEL by the BUILDER and acceptance thereof by the BUYER.

3. Documents to be Delivered to BUYER :

Upon delivery and acceptance of the VESSEL, the BUILDER shall deliver to the BUYER the following documents, which shall accompany the PROTOCOL OF DELIVERY AND ACCEPTANCE:

(a) PROTOCOL OF TRIALS of the VESSEL made pursuant to the Specifications.

(b) PROTOCOL OF INVENTORY of the equipment of the VESSEL, including spare parts and the like, all as specified in the Specifications.

(c) PROTOCOL OF STORES OF CONSUMABLE NATURE referred to under Paragraph 3(b) of Article VI hereof, including the original purchase price thereof.

(d) ALL CERTIFICATES including the BUILDER'S CERITIFICATE required to be furnished upon delivery of the VESSEL pursuant to this Contract and the Specifications. It is agreed that if, through no fault on the part of the BUILDER, the classification and /or other certificates are not available at the time of delivery of the VESSEL, provisional certificates shall be accepted by the BUYER, provided that the BUILDER shall furnish the BUYER with the formal certificates as promptly as possible after such formal certificates have been issued.

(e) DECLARATION OF WARRANTY of the BUILDER that the VESSEL is delivered to the BUYER free and clear of any liens, charges, claims, mortgages, or other encumbrances upon the BUYER'S title thereto, and in particular, that the VESSEL is absolutely free of all burdens in the nature of imports, taxes or charges imposed by the Japanese governmental authorities, as well as of all liabilities arising from the operation of the VESSEL in trial runs, or otherwise, prior to delivery.

(f) DRAWINGS AND PLANS pertaining to the VESSEL as stipulated in the Specifications.

(g) COMMERCIAL INVOICE.

4. Tender of VESSEL :

If the BUYER fails to take delivery of the VESSEL after completion thereof according to this Contract and the Specifications without any justifiable reason, the BUILDER shall have the right to tender delivery of the VESSEL after compliance with all procedural requirements as above provided.

5. Title and Risk :

Title to and risk of loss of the VESSEL shall pass to the BUYER only upon delivery and acceptance thereof having been completed as stated above; it being expressly understood that, until such delivery is effected, title to and risk of loss of the VESSEL and her equipment shall be in the BUILDER. Excepting risks of war, earthquakes and tidal waves.

6. Removal of VESSEL :

The BUYER shall take possession of the VESSEL immediately upon delivery and acceptance thereof and shall remove the VESSEL from the premises of the Shipyard within three (3) days after delivery and acceptance thereof is effected. If the BUYER shall not remove the VESSEL from the premises of the Shipyard within the aforesaid three (3) days, then, in such event the BUYER shall pay to the BUILDER the reasonable mooring charges of the VESSEL.

ARTICLE VII – EXPLANATION

SAJ Form under this article prescribes for the delivery of the vessel from the builder to the buyer.

According to Section 19 of the Indian Sale of Goods Act, 1930 the property passes when intended to pass. Section 19(1) states that where there is a contract for the sale of specific or ascertained goods the property in them is transferred to the buyer at such time as the parties to the contract intend it to be transferred. Section 19(2) states that for the purpose of ascertaining the intention of the parties regard shall be had to the terms of the contract, the conduct of the parties and the circumstances of the case. Section 19(3) states that unless a different intention appears, the rules contained in sections 20 to 24 are rules for ascertaining the intention of the parties as to the time at which the property in the goods is to pass to the buyer.

Time and Place

It is decided in this contract when and where the vessel will be delivered by the builder to the buyer. Ship building is a massive project as explained earlier and it is normal that the given time frame may not be sufficient to complete the project before the agreed date. However, this date is agreed, giving a time frame to the builder to complete the project. The builder would definitely agree to such date basis their past experience of construction of such vessel. The agreed date can be extended in the event of delays as mentioned in the contract such as Force Majeure and permissible delays. Such date including the extended date is called the Delivery Date.

When and How Effected

Once the buyer and the builder have fulfilled all their obligations under the contract, the delivery of the vessel will be effected by the concurrent delivery by each of the parties to the other of the PROTOCOL OF DELIVERY AND ACCEPTANCE, which is basically acknowledgement of the delivery of the vessel by the builder and acceptance of the delivery by the buyer.

Documents to be delivered to BUYER

The following documents shall be delivered by the builder to the buyer upon delivery and acceptance of the vessel. These documents shall delivered alongwith the PROTOCOL OF DELIVERY AND ACCEPTANCE:
(a) PROTOCOL OF TRIALS of the vessel

Under Article VI, the detailed result of the trials are submitted by the builder to the buyer. The details have been discussed in the explanation of Article VI.

(b) PROTOCOL OF INVENTORY of the equipment of the VESSEL

This gives the list of machinery and equipment installed on the vessel including the spare parts, all as specified in the Specifications.

(c) PROTOCOL OF STORES OF CONSUMABLE NATURE

This gives the list of stores of consumable nature that is referred to under Paragraph 3(b) of Article VI, including the original purchase price. This also includes the fuel oil, lubricating oil and greases. The final quantity is checked and confirmed by representatives of both buyer and builder. This will be used for final calculation of the cost which to be borne by the buyer as agreed.

(d) ALL CERTIFICATES

All the vessel certificates, statutory classification and trading, including the BUILDER'S CERITIFICATE are required to be furnished upon delivery of the vessel according the provisions of the contract and the specifications. In case the certificates are not presented at the time of the delivery of the vessel then provisional certificates shall be accepted by the buyer provided that the builder presents the formal certificates as soon as they are issued.

BUILDER'S CERTIFICATE OR BILL OF SALE

This is a crucial document which will be needed by the buyer in order to register the vessel with the flag state authorities upon delivery. It is formal evidence that the title of the vessel is transferred to the buyer by the builder.

(e) DECLARATION OF WARRANTY

This is basically a declaration by the builder that the vessel is being delivered to the buyer free and clear of any liens, charges, claims, mortgages, or other encumbrances, and that the vessel is in particular, absolutely free of all burdens in the nature of imports, taxes or charges imposed by the governmental authorities, as well as of all liabilities arising from the operation of the vessel in trial runs, or otherwise, prior to the delivery. It also includes all the subcontracted work which had been carried out prior to the delivery, which would mean that it is also clear of all the liabilities of the Builder to its sub-contractors, employees and crew.

(f) DRAWINGS AND PLANS

All the drawings and plans pertaining to the VESSEL and as stipulated in the specifications are to be handed over to the buyer by the builder. Usually 3 complete sets of drawings and plans are submitted but may vary according to the agreement between the parties. Usually, one master copy will be in the possession of the Master of the vessel, the second copy will be used by the vessel crew whilst the third copy will be with the buyer at their technical office.

(g) COMMERCIAL INVOICE

This commercial invoice basically shows the break down of payments made towards the purchase of vessel, detailing the amounts paid in instalments, adjustments made to the price and final adjusted contract price.

Tender of VESSEL

Once the vessel has been completed in accordance to the contract and specifications, if the buyer fails to take delivery of the vessel without justifiable reasons, the builder shall have the right to tender delivery of the vessel after having complied with the procedural requirements as explained above.

According to Section 36(4) of the Indian Sale of Goods Act, 1930 the demand or tender of delivery may be treated as ineffectual unless made at a reasonable hour. What is a reasonable hour is a question of fact.

Further Section 44 of the Act, prescribes for liability of buyer for neglecting or refusing delivery of goods. It states that when the seller is ready and willing to deliver the goods and requests the buyer to take delivery, and the buyer does not within a reasonable time after such request take delivery of the goods, he is liable to the seller for any loss occasioned by his neglect or refusal to take delivery and also for reasonable charge for the care and custody of the goods; provided that nothing in this section shall affect the rights of the seller where the neglect or refusal of the buyer to take delivery amounts to a repudiation of the contract.

Title and Risk

SAJ form states clearly that the title and risk remains with the builder until the vessel has been delivered and accepted by the buyer. Once the procedural requirements have been followed and the buyer takes delivery of the vessel, the title and risk immediately shifts to the buyer. Until the delivery takes place in accordance to the contract and the specifications, the title and risk of loss of the vessel and her equipment remains with the builder except in case of risk of war, earthquake and tidal waves.

Section 26 of the Indian Sale of Goods Act, 1930 prescribes that the risk prima facie passes with the property. It states that unless agreed, the goods remain at the seller's risk until the property therein is transferred to the buyer, but when the property therein is transferred to the buyer, the goods are at the buyer's risk whether delivery has been made or not; provided that, where delivery has been delayed through the fault of either buyer or seller, the goods are at the risk of the party in fault as regards any loss which might not have occurred but for such fault; Provided also that nothing in this section shall affect the duties or liabilities of either seller or buyer as bailee of the goods of the other party.

Removal of VESSEL

Once the buyer has taken delivery of the vessel and has accepted the vessel in accordance to the contract and specifications, the buyer shall take possession of the vessel immediately. The buyer should then remove the vessel from the premises of the builder's shipyard within three (3) days after delivery and acceptance. If the buyer does not remove the vessel from the premises of the builder's shipyard within the stipulated three (3) days, then the buyer shall pay to the builder charges for keeping the vessel at the shipyard. The builder ought to charge the buyer reasonably for keeping the vessel moored at the shipyard.

ARTICLE VIII – DELAYS AND EXTENSION OF TIME FOR DELIVERY (FORCE MAJEURE)

1. Causes of Delay :

If, at any time before the actual delivery, either the construction of the VESSEL or any performance required as a prerequisite of delivery of the VESSEL is delayed due to Acts of God, acts of princes or rulers, intervention of government authorities, war, blockade, revolution, insurrections, mobilization, civil commotion, riots, strikes, sabotages, lockouts, labour shortages, plague, epidemics, fire, flood, typhoons, hurricanes, storms or other weather conditions not included in normal planning, earthquakes, tidal waves, landslides, explosions, collisions, strandings, embargoes, delays in transportation, shortage of materials or equipment, or delay in delivery or inability to take delivery thereof, provided that such materials and equipment at the time of ordering could reasonably be expected by the BUILDER to be delivered in time, prolonged failure or restriction of energy sources including electric current and petroleum, mishaps of casting and /or forging; or by destruction of the Shipyard or works of the BUILDER or its subcontractors, or of the VESSEL or any part thereof by fire, flood, or other causes as above specified; or due to delays in the BUILDER'S other commitments resulting from any such causes hereinabove described which in turn delay the construction of the VESSEL or the BUILDER'S performance under this Contract; or due to other causes or accidents beyond control of the BUILDER, its subcontractors or supplier of the nature whether or not indicated by the foregoing words, irrespective of whether or not these events could be foreseen at the day of signing this Contract, the Delivery Date shall be postponed for a period of time which shall not exceed the total accumulated time of all such delays.

2. Notice of Delay :

Within seven (7) days from the date of commencement of the delay on account of which the BUILDER claims that it is entitled under this Contract to a postponement of the Delivery Date of the VESSEL, the BUILDER shall advise the BUYER by cable confirmed in writing of the date such delay commences and the reasons therefor.
Likewise, within seven (7) days after such delay ends, the BUILDER shall advise the BUYER in writing or by cable confirmed in writing of the date such delay ended, and also shall specify the period of time by which the Delivery Date is postponed by reason of such delay. Failure of the BUYER to acknowledge the BUILDER'S notification of any claim for postponement of the Delivery Date within seven (7) days after receipt of such notification shall be deemed to be a waiver by the BUYER of its right to object to such postponement.

3. Definition of Permissible Delay :

Delays on account of such causes as specified in Paragraph 1 of this Article and any other delays of a nature which under the terms of this Contract permits postponement of the Delivery Date shall be understood to be permissible delays and are to be distinguished from unauthorized delays on account of which the Contract Price is subject to adjustment as provided for in Article III hereof.

4. **Right to Rescind for Excessive Delay :**

If the total accumulated time of all delays on account of the causes specified in Paragraph 1 of this Article, excluding delays of a nature which, under the terms of this Contract, permit postponement of the Delivery Date, amounts to Two Hundred and Ten (210) days or more, then, in such event, the BUYER may rescind this Contract in accordance with the provisions of Article X hereof. The BUILDER may, at any time after the accumulated time of the aforementioned delays justifying rescission by the BUYER, demand in writing that the BUYER shall, within twenty (20) days after such demand is received by the BUYER, either notify the BUILDER of its intention to rescind this Contract, or consent to a postponement of the Delivery Date to a specific future date; it being understood and agreed by the parties hereto that, if any further delay occurs on account of causes justifying rescission as specified in this Article, the BUYER shall have the same right of rescission upon the same terms as hereinabove provided.

ARTICLE VIII – EXPLANATION

It is not always possible to finish such a massive project exactly as per predicted schedule. Even after having allowed for some predicted delays such as for observed defects and rectification after the trials, there may be instances when the project may be stalled due to reasons beyond the control of the builder. The inevitable takes place even with the builder having taken reasonable care and precaution and could not have foreseen the inevitable. Section 56 of the Indian Contract Act, 1872 states that a contract to do an act which, after the contract is made, becomes impossible or, by reason of some event which the promisor could not prevent, unlawful, becomes void when the act becomes impossible or unlawful. SAJ Form under this article prescribes for the delays and extension of time for delivery due to Force Majeure.

Causes of Delay

The form lists out about thirty five causes of delay that may take place before the actual delivery of the vessel, during the course of construction of the vessel or any performance required as a prerequisite of delivery of the vessel.
Acts of God, flood, typhoons, hurricanes, storms or other weather conditions, earthquakes, tidal waves, landslides, plague, epidemics. Some of the listed causes do come under Acts of God, however, the SAJ form specifies it separately to ensure there is no ambiguity. Under

the Indian context suggest the readers to be aware of the 'Rule of Strict liability'[26] and the 'Rule of Absolute liability'[27].

Acts of princes or rulers, intervention of government authorities, war, blockade, revolution, insurrections, mobilization, civil commotion, riots, strikes, sabotages, lockouts, labour shortages, fire, embargoes.

We frequently see the economic blockade to nations not following the rule of international law by the world body or even between the regional countries within their own regional cooperation councils.

Workers union differences with shipyard management is one of the most common causes for delays in construction of the vessel. Workers very often seek to improve their working conditions, wages, terms and conditions with the employer. Failure of which a strike becomes imminent.

'Rioting' means whenever force or violence is used by an unlawful assembly, or by any member thereof, in prosecution of the common object of such assembly, every member of such assembly is guilty of the offence of rioting[28].

The Industrial Disputes Act, 1947 of India defines 'strike' as a cessation of work by a body of persons employed in any industry acting in combination, or a concerned refusal, or a refusal under a common understanding, of any number of persons who are or have been so employed to continue to work or to accept employment[29].

The 'lockout' means the temporary closing of a place of employment, or the suspension of work, or the refusal by an employer to continue to employ any number of persons employed by him[30].

Delays in transportation of materials or equipment, shortage of materials or equipment, or delay in delivery of them or inability to take delivery of them, provided that such materials and equipment at the time of ordering could reasonably be expected by the builder to have been delivered in time.

Continuous, frequent failure of energy source or restriction of the energy source due to shortages or no supply. Energy source such as electric current and petroleum.

Other causes mentioned in the SAJ form are mishaps of casting and or forging, or by destruction of the shipyard or works of the builder or its subcontractors, or of the vessel or any part thereof by fire, flood, or other causes as explained above and specified in the form.

Delays in the builder's other commitments resulting from any of the causes specified in this article of the SAJ form, which then results in further delay of the construction of the vessel or the builder's performance under this contract.

The SAJ form further mentions 'other causes' or accidents which are beyond the control of the builder, its subcontractors or supplier of the nature whether or not indicated by the

---

[26] Rylands v Fletcher, 1868, L.R. 3 H.L. 330.

[27] MC Mehta v Union of India, A.I.R. 1987 S.C. 1086.
  Union Carbide Corporation v Union of India, A.I.R. 1992 S.C. 248.

[28] The Indian Penal Code, 1860, Chapter VIII, Section 146.

[29] The Industrial Disputes Act, 1947, Chapter 1 Section (2)(q).

[30] Ibid, Chapter 1 Section (2)(l).

foregoing words of the article, irrespective of whether or not these events could be foreseen at the day of signing the contract, the delivery date shall be postponed for a period of time which shall not exceed the total accumulated time of all such delays.

Notice of Delay

The builder must notify the buyer within seven days from the date of commencement of the delays as have been mentioned in this article and explained above. In the notice the builder must mention the reason for the delay for which he is entitled under the contract to postpone the delivery of the vessel and the date of commencement of the delay.

Once the delay as mentioned in the notice has ended, the builder must notify the buyer within seven days that such delay has ended. The builder shall also mention the period of time by which the delivery date is postponed.

Failure on the part of the buyer to acknowledge receipt of the builder's notice of postponement of delivery of vessel within seven days after receipt of such notification shall be deemed to be a waiver by the buyer of its right to object postponement of delivery date by the builder.

Definition of Permissible Delay

The SAJ form defines permissible delay. The delay due to the causes (Force Majeure) specified in this article and allowed under the terms of the contract are called permissible delays. Permissible delays in simple words would mean the delays that are permitted under the contract for which there will be no adjustment to the contract price. Any unauthorized delays will result in adjustment to the contract price as provided in Article III.

Right to Rescind for Excessive Delay

The SAJ form provides the buyer the right to rescind the contract for excessive delays even for the permissible delays under this article. It mentions that where the total accumulated time of delay due to the causes specified in this article (Force Majeure) amounts to two hundred and ten (210) days or more, then the buyer may rescind the contract in accordance with provisions of Article X of the form. After such elapse of time, the builder may demand in writing from the buyer within twenty (20) days whether the buyer intends to rescind the contract or consents to further postponement of the delivery date to a specific future date.

ARTICLE IX – WARRANTY OF QUALITY

1. Guarantee :

Subject to the provisions hereinafter set forth, the BUILDER undertakes to remedy, free of charge to the BUYER, any defects in the VESSEL which are due to defective material and/or bad workmanship on the part of the BUILDER and/or its sub-contractors, provided that the defects are discovered within a period of twelve (12) months after the date of delivery of the VESSEL and a notice thereof is duly given to the BUILDER as hereinabove provided.   For the purpose of this Article, the VESSEL shall include her hull, machinery, equipment and gear, but excludes any parts for the VESSEL which have been supplied by or on behalf of the BUYER.

2. Notice of Defects :

The BUYER shall notify the BUILDER in writing, or by cable confirmed in writing, of any defects for which claim is made under this guarantee as promptly as possible after discovery thereof. The BUYER'S written notice shall describe the nature and extent of the defects. The BUILDER shall have no obligation for any defects discovered prior to the expiry date of the said twelve (12) months period, unless notice of such defects is received by the BUILDER not later than thirty (30) days after such expiry date.

3. Remedy of Defects :

(a) The BUILDER shall remedy, at its expense, any defects, against which the VESSEL is guaranteed under this Article, by making all necessary repairs or replacements at the Shipyard.

(b) However, if it is impractical to bring the VESSEL to the Shipyard, the BUYER may cause the necessary repairs or replacement to be made elsewhere which is deemed suitable for the purpose, provided that, in such event, the BUILDER may forward or supply replacement parts or materials to the VESSEL, unless forwarding or supplying thereof to the VESSEL would impair or delay the operation or working schedule of the VESSEL. In the event that the BUYER proposes to cause the necessary repairs or replacements to be made to the VESSEL at any other shipyard or works than the Shipyard, the BUYER shall first, but in all events as soon as possible, give the BUILDER notice in writing or by cable confirmed in writing of the time and place such repairs will be made, and if the VESSEL is not thereby delayed, or her operation or working schedule is not thereby impaired, the BUILDER shall have the right to verify by its own representative(s) the nature and extents of the defects complained of. The BUILDER shall, in such case, promptly advise the BUYER by cable, after such examination has been completed, of its acceptance or rejection of the defects as ones that are covered by the guarantee herein provided. Upon the BUILDER'S acceptance of the of the defects as justifying remedy under this Article, or upon award of the arbitration so determining, the BUILDER shall immediately pay to the BUYER for such repairs or replacements a sum equal to the reasonable cost of making the same repairs or replacements in the Shipyard.

(c) In any case, the VESSEL, shall be taken at the BUYER'S cost and responsibility to the place elected, ready in all respects for such repairs or replacements.

(d) Any dispute under this Article shall be referred to arbitration in accordance with the provisions of Article XIII hereof.

4. Extent of BUILDER's Responsibility :

(a) The BUILDER shall have no responsibility or liability for any other defects whatsoever in the VESSEL than the defects specified in Paragraph 1 of this Article. Nor the BUILDER shall in any circumstances be responsible or liable for any consequential or special losses, damages or expenses including, but not limited to, loss of time, loss of profit or earning or demurrage directly or indirectly occasioned to the BUYER by reason of the defects specified in Paragraph 1 of this Article or due to repairs or other works done to the VESSEL to remedy such defects.

(b) The BUILDER shall not be responsible for any defects in any part of the VESSEL which may subsequent to delivery of the VESSEL have been replaced or in any way repaired by any other contractor, or for any defects which have been caused or aggravated by omission or improper use and maintenance of the VESSEL on the part of the BUYER, its servants or agents or by ordinary wear and tear or by any other circumstances whatsoever beyond the control of the BUILDER.

(c) The guarantee, contained as hereinabove in this Article replaces and excludes any other liability, guarantee, warranty and/or condition imposed or implied by the law, customary, statutory or otherwise, by reason of the construction and sale of the VESSEL for and to the BUYER.

5. Guarantee Engineer :

The BUILDER shall have the right to appoint a Guarantee Engineer to serve on the VESSEL as its representative for such portion of the guarantee period as the BUILDER may decide. The BUYER and its employees shall give the Guarantee Engineer full cooperation in carrying out his duties as the representative of the BUILDER on board the VESSEL. The BUYER shall accord the Guarantee Engineer the treatment comparable to the VESSEL'S Chief Engineer and shall provide him with accommodations and subsistence at no cost of [sic] the BUILDER and/or the Guarantee Engineer.
The BUYER shall pay to the BUILDER the sum of ....per month as a compensation for a part of costs and charges to be borne by the BUILDER in connection with the Guarantee Engineer and also shall pay the expenses of repatriation to Tokyo, Japan, by air upon termination of his service.
Pertaining to the detailed particulars of the Paragraph, an agreement will be made according to this effect between the parties hereto upon delivery of the VESSEL.

ARTICLE IX – EXPLANATION

Ship construction is a very expensive project. It was explained under Article VII that the title and risk remains with the builder until the vessel has been delivered and accepted by the buyer. After builder delivers the vessel to the buyer and it is accepted by the buyer, the title and risk of the vessel shifts from the builder to the buyer.

The builder will try to minimize his responsibility after the vessel has been delivered to the buyer, namely in regards to the defects found in the vessel after delivery. On the other hand, the buyer will try to keep the responsibility of the builder to ensure that it will not effect his business, namely in regards to the defects found in the vessel after delivery of the vessel.

In order to resolve the stand of both parties, most ship building contracts will include the warranty of quality. Normally a time period of twelve months after the delivery of the vessel is given to the buyer, wherein the buyer reports any defects found during this period to the builder. The builder will ensure to correct the defects found during this warranty period at his own cost.

Let us now discuss the provisions set out in the SAJ form under this article.

Guarantee

Under the SAJ form, the builder takes responsibility to correct the defects found in the vessel due to defective material, bad workmanship of his own workers or of the sub-contractors. Such defects should be discovered and notified by the buyer to the builder within a time period of twelve months after the delivery of the vessel. The form further clarifies that the following are included in the term 'Vessel':

Hull

Machinery

Equipment and gear

It does not include any part of the vessel which has been supplied by the buyer.

Notice of Defects

Whenever any defects are discovered in the vessel during the warranty period, the buyer shall notify the builder as promptly as possible. The notice should outline the nature and extent of the defect. The builder will not have any obligation for defects that are discovered before the expiry of the warranty period, unless the builder receives notice of the defect from the buyer which should be not later than thirty days from expiry date of the warranty period.

Remedy of Defects

After the defects have been discovered and duly notified by the buyer to the builder, the builder shall carry out necessary repairs or provide replacement of the equipment for which the vessel is guaranteed at the shipyard.

The vessel after delivery and acceptance of the buyer is put into service by the buyer as per his business plan. Some buyers carry on the business on their own with their inhouse commercial and technical teams whereas some buyers lease the vessel to companies, charterers that provide regular income to the owner.

During the warranty period, whilst the vessel is trading it will be difficult and impractical to bring the vessel to the builder's shipyard for repairs. For example, the vessel is trading in the wider Caribbean region whilst the shipyard where the vessel was constructed is in Japan. The buyer may seek to carry out the necessary repairs or replacement to be carried out elsewhere which is suitable for the purpose. In such case, the builder may forward the replacement parts or materials to the vessel unless it impairs or delays the operation or working schedule of the vessel.

In case the buyer proposes to the builder to carry out the necessary repairs or replacements to be made to the vessel at any other shipyard, then the buyer must notify the builder as soon as possible confirming the time and place of such repairs to be made to the vessel. The builder shall have the right to verify the nature and extent of the defect by its representatives. The builder will send its representatives to such place and time as agreed by the buyer without causing delay or impairing the vessel schedule or her operations. After the examination of the defects reported by the buyer, the builder shall promptly report to the buyer of its acceptance or rejection of the defects.

Further, once the builder accepts the defects as notified by the buyer and as justified remedy under this article or as awarded following an arbitration, the builder shall pay the buyer immediately for the repairs or replacements of materials. The payment should be a sum which is equal to the reasonable cost of making the same repairs or replacements in the shipyard.

The SAJ form further mentions that the vessel will be taken to the place as agreed for the repairs or replacements of materials at the buyer's cost and responsibility.

The form provides for dispute arising under this article to be referred to arbitration in accordance with provisions of Article XIII.

Extent of builder's responsibility

As explained earlier, after builder delivers the vessel to the buyer and it is accepted by the buyer, the title and risk of the vessel is transferred from the builder to the buyer.

The SAJ form makes it clear that the builder shall have no responsibility or liability for any other defects in the vessel other than the defects which are specified in paragraph 1 of this article. Also the builder shall not be responsible or liable for any losses, damages or expenses, loss of time, loss of profit or earning or demurrage suffered by the buyer by reason of defects specified in paragraph 1 of this article or due to repairs or any work carried out on the vessel to rectify the defects.

The builder will not take responsibility for any defects during the warranty period which have been attended to, repaired, replaced by any other contractor. As explained earlier in this article, the builder will first inspect, examine the defects after duly being notified by the buyer and then take necessary action. The builder will not entertain a third party carrying out the repairs or replacement without its prior approval.

The builder will not take responsibility for any defects during the warranty period which have been caused, aggravated due to incorrect operation, usage and maintenance of the vessel on the part of the buyer, its servants or agents, basically the crew of the vessel or by ordinary wear and tear or by any other circumstances which are beyond the control of the builder.

Guarantee Engineer

During the period of guarantee, the builder reserves the right to place an engineer onboard the vessel as its representative for such period as the builder may decide. Such representative is called the guarantee engineer. The buyer, its employees, basically the crew of the vessel, should treat the guarantee engineer as comparable to the vessel's chief engineer and provide him with cabin and subsistence at no cost to the builder or to the guarantee engineer. The guarantee engineer shall be given full cooperation by the buyer and its employees, basically the crew of the vessel in order to carry out his duties as the representative of the builder onboard the vessel.

ARTICLE X – RESCISSION BY BUYER

1. Notice :

The payments made by the BUYER prior to the delivery of the vessel shall be in the nature of advances to the BUILDER. In the event that the BUYER shall exercise its right of rescission of this Contract under and pursuant to any of the provisions of this Contract specifically permitting the BUYER to do so, then the BUYER shall notify the BUILDER in writing or by cable confirmed in writing, and such rescission shall be effective as of the date notice thereof is received by the BUILDER.

2. Refund by BUILDER :

Thereupon the BUILDER shall promptly refund to the BUYER the full amount of all sums paid by the BUYER to the BUILDER on account of the VESSEL, unless the BUILDER proceeds to the arbitration under the provisions of Article XIII hereof.
In such event, the BUILDER shall pay the BUYER interest at the rate of ……………..
……….. percent (…………………%) per annum on the amount required herein to be refunded to the BUYER, computed from the respective dates on which such sums were paid by the BUYER to the BUILDER to the date of remittance by transfer of such refund to the BUYER by the BUILDER, provided, however, that if the said rescission by the BUYER is made under the provisions of Paragraph 4 of Article VIII hereof, then in such event the BUILDER shall not be required to pay any interest.

3. Discharge of Obligations :

Upon such refund by the BUILDER to the BUYER, all obligations, duties and liabilities of each of the parties hereto to the other under this Contract shall be forthwith completely discharged.

ARTICLE X – EXPLANATION

This article provides for rescission of the contract by the buyer pursuant to the provisions of the contract which specifically permits the buyer to rescind the contract. As was explained under Article II, method of payment of contract price, the buyer pays various installments under certain stages and milestones before delivery of the vessel. This helps both the parties commit themselves to the huge project. Whilst the buyer having paid huge amount upfront would be interested in completion of the project duly, it also gives the builder funds to start the project which is quite expensive whereby the builder has to fund not only the materials but also the workmanship. Mostly a buyer would have taken funds on credit from banks or investment partners and thereby exposes himself to financial credit risk right at the beginning of the project and before delivery of the vessel. Hence it is vital on the part of the buyer to secure his interests and be able to claim the funds back from the builder in case the builder fails to fulfill his obligations under the provisions of the contract.

Section 62 of the Indian Contract Act, 1872 prescribes the effect of novation, rescission and alteration of contract. It states that if the parties to a contract agree to […] rescind […], the original contract, need not be performed.

For specific performance in the Indian context, the laws are contained in section 9 to 25 of *The Specific Relief Act, 1963* and section 58 of the *Sale of Goods Act, 1930*. Specific performance is based on equitable principle. When one party to the contract fails to perform his part of the contract, then the other party may seek specific performance of the contract. Section 10 of *The Specific Relief Act, 1963* prescribes for cases in which specific performance of contract is enforceable. The specific performance of any contract may be enforced, only in the discretion of the hon'ble court and in following cases:

(a) When there exists no standard for ascertaining actual damage caused by the non-performance of the act agreed to be done, or

(b) When the act agreed to be done is such that compensation in money for its non-performance would not afford adequate relief.

Section 58 of the *Sale of Goods Act, 1930* prescribes for specific performance at the discretion of the court, if it thinks fit, on the application of the plaintiff, by its decree direct that the contract shall be performed specifically, without giving the defendant the option of retaining the goods on payment of damages. The decree may be unconditional, or upon such terms and conditions as to damages, payment of the price, or otherwise, as the Court may deem just.

Notice

When the buyer invokes his right to rescind the contract pursuant to any of the provisions of the contract which permits the buyer to rescind the contract, then the buyer shall notify the builder in writing. The notice of rescission will be effective on the date it is received by the builder.

Refund by builder

After receiving the notice of rescission, the builder shall promptly refund the buyer. The amount to be refunded is the full amount of all sums which have been paid by the buyer to the builder on account of the vessel. The builder could also proceed with arbitration under the provisions of Article XIII if he disputes the refund.

Discharge of Obligations

After the builder has refunded the buyer, all obligations, duties and liabilities of both the parties under the contract towards each other is completely discharged.

ARTICLE XI – BUYER'S DEFAULT

1. Definition of Default :

The BUYER shall be deemed to be in default of performance of its obligations under this Contract in the following cases:

(a) If the BUYER fails to pay any of the First, Second and Third Installments to the BUILDER within three (3) days after such Installment becomes due and payable under the provisions of Article II hereof; or

(b) If the BUYER fails to pay the Fourth Installment to the BUILDER concurrently with the delivery of the VESSEL by the BUILDER to the BUYER as provided in Article II hereof; or

(c) If the BUYER fails to take delivery of the VESSEL, when the VESSEL is duly tendered for delivery by the BUILDER under the provisions of Article VII hereof.

2. Interest and Charge :

If the BUYER is in default to payment as to any Installment as provided in Paragraph (a) and (b) of this Article, the BUYER shall pay interest on such Installment at the rate of .... percent (...................%) per annum from the due date thereof to the date of payment to the BUILDER of the full amount including interest; in case the BUYER shall fail to take delivery of the VESSEL as provided in Paragraph 1 (c) of this Article, the BUYER shall be deemed in default of payment of the Fourth Installment and shall pay interest thereon at the same rate as aforesaid from and including the day on which the VESSEL is tendered for delivery by the BUILDER.

In any event of default by the BUYER, the BUYER shall also pay all charges and expenses incurred by the BUILDER in consequence of such default.

3. Effect of Default :

(a) If any default by the BUYER occurs as provided hereinbefore, the Delivery Date shall be automatically postponed for a period of continuance of such default by the BUYER.

(b) If any default by the BUYER continues for a period of fifteen (15) days, the BUILDER may, at its option, rescind this Contract by giving notice of such effect to the BUYER by cable confirmed in writing. Upon receipt by the BUYER of such notice of rescission, this Contract shall forthwith become null and void and any of the BUYER'S Supplies shall become the sole property of the BUILDER.

In the event of such rescission of this Contract, the BUILDER shall be entitled to retain any Installment or Installments theretofore paid by the BUYER to the BUILDER on account of this Contract.

4. **Sale of Vessel :**

   (a) In the event of rescission of this Contract as above provided, the BUILDER shall have full right and power either to complete or not to complete the VESSEL as it deems fit, and to sell the VESSEL at a public or private sale on such terms and conditions as the BUILDER thinks fit without being answerable for any loss or damage.

   (b) In the event of the sale of the VESSEL in its completed state, the proceeds of the sale received by the BUILDER shall be applied firstly to payment of all expenses attending such sale and otherwise incurred by the BUILDER as a result of the BUYER'S default, and then to payment of all unpaid Installments of the Contract Price and interest on such Installments at the rate of …………….. percent (…………..%) per annum from the respective due dates thereof to the date of application.

   (c) In the event of the sale of the VESSEL in its incompleted state, the proceeds of the sale received by the BUILDER shall be applied firstly to all expenses attending such sale and otherwise incurred by the BUILDER as a result of the BUYER'S default, and then to payment of all costs of construction of the VESSEL less the Installments so retained by the BUILDER and compensation to the BUILDER for a reasonable loss of profit due to the rescission of this Contract.

   (d) In either of the above events of sale, if the proceeds of sale exceeds the total of amounts to which such proceeds are to be applied as aforesaid, the BUILDER shall promptly pay the excess to the BUYER without interest, provided, however, that the amount of such payment to the BUYER shall in no event exceed the total amount of Installments already paid by the BUYER and the cost of the BUYER'S Supplies, if any.

   (e) If the proceeds of sale are insufficient to pay such total amounts payable as aforesaid, the BUYER shall promptly pay the deficiency to the BUILDER upon request.

ARTICLE XI – EXPLANATION

This article lays down provision for the buyer's default. It defines the term default. It provides for interest and charges that will be applicable to the buyer in default of the payment of any installment. It further provides for the effect of buyer's default to the postponement of the delivery date of the vessel and possible rescission of the contract by the builder pursuant to the provisions of the contract. After rescission of the contract by the builder, it provides for the sale of the vessel.

Definition of Default

The SAJ form defines the default of the buyer in relation to his performance of his obligations under the contract in the following cases:

(a) When the buyer fails to pay the builder any of the installments, first or second or third installment within three days of their due date when such installment becomes payable in accordance with the provisions of Article II;

(b) When the buyer fails to pay the builder the fourth installment. This installment is due to be paid upon delivery of the vessel by the builder to the buyer in accordance with the provisions of Article II; or

(c) When the buyer fails to take delivery of the vessel. The vessel by the builder has been duly tendered for delivery to the buyer in accordance with the provisions of Article VII.

Interest and Charge

This clause is inserted to have interest and charges payable for the defaulted installments payable. It is an agreed rate of percent per annum payable on the installment from the due date when the installment is payable to the date when the installment alongwith with the interest is paid to the builder.

This clause also treats the failure of the buyer to take delivery of the vessel as if it is default in the payment of the fourth installment. Similarly, the buyer will have to pay the above agreed rate of percent per annum payable on the fourth installment from the due date when the vessel is tendered for delivery by the builder.
Further, whatever charges and expenses are incurred by the builder due to the buyer's default as explained above, then the buyer shall pay such charges and expenses to the builder.

Effect of Default

This article takes effect after the buyer's default, there is no requirement as per the SAJ form for any kind of notice of default which is to be tendered by the builder to the buyer so as to seek remedy for the buyer's default.

(a) The delivery date of the vessel shall be automatically postponed for a period which is the date from which the buyer's default start until it ceases.

(b) When the buyer's default extends for a period of fifteen days, then the builder has the option of rescinding the contract. In order to rescind the contract, the builder has to give notice of rescission in writing to the buyer. When the buyer receives the notice of rescission from the builder, then the contract becomes null and void.

Any of the buyer's supplies becomes the sole property of the builder. The buyer may have supplied machinery, equipment as to his requirement and it will be important to mention such transfer to the builder to avoid claims for such machinery, equipment by the buyer.

The builder will also be entitled to retain any of the installment or installments that have been paid by the buyer to the builder.

Sale of Vessel

(a) When the rescission of contract takes place as explained above, the builder will then have the right and power firstly to either complete or not complete the construction of the vessel as it deems fit.

Secondly, the builder shall have the right to sell the vessel either publicly or privately on such terms and conditions as the builder thinks fit without being answerable for any loss or damage.

(b) The SAJ form first deals with the sale of the vessel in its completed state. It provides that when such completed vessel is sold, the proceeds of the sale received by the builder shall first be applied towards payment of all the expenses that have been incurred by the builder for such sale and otherwise incurred by the builder as a result of the buyer's default. The proceeds of the sale will then be applied towards payment of all unpaid installments of the contract price and interest payable at the agreed rate of percent per annum from the due date to the date of application.

(c) The SAJ form next deals with the sale of the vessel in its incomplete state. When the vessel is sold in its incompleted state, the proceeds of the sale received by the builder shall first be applied towards payment of all the expenses that have been incurred by the builder for such sale and otherwise incurred by the builder as a result of the buyer's default. The proceeds of the sale will then be applied towards payment of all costs of construction of the vessel minus the installments which have been retained by the builder and the compensation to the builder for a reasonable loss of profit due to the rescission of the contract.

(d) After the sale of the vessel, if the proceeds of the sale exceeds the amount payable to the builder, then the builder shall pay the excess amount to the buyer promptly and without interest. It is to be noted that this amount which is payable to the buyer shall in no event exceed the total amount of installments already paid by the buyer and the cost of the buyer's supplies.

(e) After the sale of the vessel, if the proceeds of the sale falls short of the amount payable to the builder, then the buyer shall pay the deficiency to the builder promptly upon request.

ARTICLE XII – INSURANCE

1. Extent of Insurance Coverage :

From the time of keel-laying of the VESSEL until the same is completed, delivered to and accepted by the BUYER, the BUILDER shall, at its own cost and expense, keep the VESSEL and all machinery, materials, equipment, appurtenances and outfit, delivered to the Shipyard for the VESSEL or built into, or installed in or upon the VESSEL, including the BUYER'S Supplies, fully insured with Japanese insurance companies under coverage corresponding to the Japanese Builder's Risks Insurance Clause.

The amount of such insurance coverage shall, up to the date of delivery of the VESSEL, be in an amount at least equal to, but not limited to, the aggregate of the payment made by the BUYER to the BUILDER including the value of the BUYER'S Supplies.

The policy referred to hereinabove shall be taken out in the name of the BUILDER and all losses under such policy shall be payable to the BUILDER.

If the BUYER so requests, the BUILDER shall at the BUYER'S cost procure insurance on the VESSEL and all parts, materials, machinery and equipment intended therefor against risks of earthquake, strikes, war peril or other risks not heretofore provided and shall make all arrangements to that end. The cost of such insurance shall be reimbursed to the BUILDER by the BUYER upon delivery of the VESSEL.

2. Application of Recovered Amount :

(a) Partial Loss:

In the event the VESSEL shall be damaged by any insured cause whatsoever prior to acceptance thereof by the BUYER and in the further event that such damage shall not constitute an actual or a constructive total loss of the VESSEL, the BUILDER shall apply the amount recovered under the insurance policy referred to in Paragraph 1 of the Article to the repair of such damage satisfactory to the Classification Society, and the BUYER shall accept the VESSEL under the Contract if completed in accordance with this Contract and Specifications.

(b) Total Loss:

However, in the event that the VESSEL is determined to be an actual or constructive total loss, the BUILDER shall by the mutual agreement between the parties hereto, either:

(i) Proceed in accordance with the terms of this Contract, in which case the amount recovered under said insurance policy shall be applied to the reconstruction of the VESSEL'S damage, provided the parties hereto shall have first agreed in writing as to such reasonable postponement of the Delivery Date and adjustment of other terms of this Contract including the Contract Price as may be necessary for the completion of such reconstruction; or

(ii) Refund immediately to the BUYER the amount of all Installments paid to the BUILDER under this Contract without any interest, whereupon this Contract shall be deemed to be rescinded and all rights, duties, liabilities and obligations

of each of the parties to the other shall terminate forthwith.
If the parties hereto fail to reach such agreement within two (2) months after the VESSEL is determined to be an actual or constructive total loss, the provisions of Sub-paragraph (b) (ii) as above shall apply.

3. **Termination of BUILDER's Obligation to Insure :**

The BUILDER'S obligation to insure the VESSEL hereunder shall cease and terminate forthwith upon delivery thereof and acceptance by the BUYER.

ARTICLE XII – EXPLANATION

This article lays down provision for the Insurance of builder's risks. Ship building is an expensive project and requires lot of investment right from the start of the project until its completion. Hence it becomes important to insure the project right from the start and during the course of the construction of the vessel. The risks exposing the project to huge loss and damages requires to be covered by insurance. The insurance seeks to cover the interest of both builder and buyer in the vessel under construction. This would come to an end once the buyer takes delivery of the vessel.

Extent of Insurance Coverage

The SAJ form under the provisions of this article provides for the extent of the insurance coverage. It mentions the period for which the insurance cover must be provided.
The period of insurance is from the time of keel-laying of vessel until the period when the vessel has been completed, delivered by the builder and duly accepted by the buyer.

During such period the builder shall, at its own cost and expense, fully insure the vessel and the following either delivered to the shipyard for the vessel or fitted in the vessel or kept onboard the vessel or built into the vessel:
Machinery
Materials
Equipment
Appurtenances and outfit
Buyer's supplies

The SAJ form requires that the builder's risks should be covered by Japanese insurance companies under coverage corresponding to the *Japanese Builder's Risks Insurance Clause.*

The SAJ form provides for the minimum amount of insurance coverage. The amount of the insurance coverage, during the insurance period i.e. from the time of keel-laying of vessel until the period when the vessel has been completed, delivered by the builder and duly accepted by the buyer, shall be an amount equal to but not limited to the aggregate of the payment that has been made by the buyer to the builder which also includes the value of the buyer's supplies.

The insurance policy shall be drawn in the name of the builder. The reason is that at this stage, the risk and title remain with the builder. Any claims towards this insurance policy cover shall be payable to the builder.

The SAJ form also provides for insurance in case the buyer requests for the cover. In case of such request from the buyer, the builder shall procure the insurance on the vessel and all parts, materials, machinery and equipment as requested. The cost of insurance such procured by the builder shall be on buyer's account. The cost of this insurance is to be reimbursed by the buyer to the builder upon delivery of the vessel. Here the form mentions the risks to be covered as earthquake, strikes, war peril or other risks.

The following are some of the key points to be noted when providing insurance cover for the vessel under construction and until delivery of the vessel takes place:
-    natural calamities such as earthquake, tsunami, tidal wave, volcanic eruption
-    war risk and civil hostility
-    strikes and lockout
-    negligence and fault of the workers
-    contractors and sub-contractors
-    risk of fire and explosion
-    pollution liability
-    launching of vessel
-    physical loss and damage
-    defects in design
-    welding defects
-    protection & indemnity
-    collision liability
-    total loss

Application of Recovered Amount

(a) For Partial Loss:
    During the insurance period i.e. from the time of keel-laying of vessel until the period when the vessel has been completed, delivered by the builder and duly accepted by the buyer, if the vessel suffers damage that is covered by the insurance, then the builder

shall apply for the amount that can be recovered under the insurance policy. The damage should not constitute actual or constructive total loss of the vessel.

The damage should be repaired to the satisfaction of the Classification Society and the buyer shall accept the vessel if it is completed in accordance to the contract and its specifications.

(b) For Total Loss:

During the insurance period, if the vessel suffers damage which is said to be an actual or constructive total loss, then the builder with mutual agreement between itself and the buyer shall either:

(i)   Use the amount recovered under the insurance policy for the covered damage towards repair of the vessel's damage. The builder and buyer shall first agree in writing the postponement of the delivery date which should be reasonable and the adjustment of other terms of the contract including the contract price as necessary for the completion of the reconstruction. OR

(ii)   Immediately refund the buyer all the amount which has been paid as installments to the builder in accordance to the terms of the contract without any interest. The contract shall then be deemed to be rescinded and all the rights, duties, liabilities and obligations of builder and buyer towards each other shall stand terminated.

If the builder and buyer fail to reach an agreement as explained above within two months after the vessel has been determined to be an actual or constructive total loss, then the provisions of sub-paragraph (b) (ii) as explained above shall be applied.

Termination of BUILDER's Obligation to Insure

The SAJ form includes the clause under this article to ensure the termination of the builder's obligation to insure the vessel upon delivery. The builder's obligation to insure the vessel ceases and terminates once the vessel is delivered by the builder to the buyer and the vessel delivery has been accepted by the buyer.

ARTICLE XIII – DISPUTE AND ARBITRATION

1. Proceedings :

In the event of any dispute between the parties hereto as to any matter arising out of or relating to this Contract or any stipulations herein or with respect which can not be settled by the parties themselves, such dispute shall be submitted to and settled by arbitration held in Tokyo, Japan, by the Japan Shipping Exchange, Inc. (hereinafter called the "Exchange") in accordance with the provisions of the Rules of Maritime Arbitration of the Exchange, except as hereinafter otherwise specifically provided.

Either party desiring to submit such dispute to the arbitration of the Exchange shall file with the Exchange the written Application for Arbitration, the Statement of Claim and the notice of appointment of an arbitrator accompanied by written acceptance of such arbitrator appointed by such party.

Within twenty (20) days after receipt of such documents as aforementioned from the Exchange, the other party shall file in turn with the Exchange the notice of appointment of an arbitrator accompanied by written acceptance of such second arbitrator appointed by the other party. These two (2) arbitrators shall be deemed, in performance of office of arbitration, as the arbitrators appointed by the Maritime Arbitrations Commission (hereinafter called the "Commission") of the Exchange.

The third arbitrator to preside over the proceedings shall be appointed by the Commission from among such persons on the Panel of Members of the Commission (or in case of particular need, from among persons not so empaneled) as have no concern whatever with the parties or in the subject of such dispute.

The three (3) arbitrators thus appointed shall constitute the board of arbitration (hereinafter called the "Arbitrations Board") for the settlement of such dispute.

In the event, however, that the said other party should fail to appoint a second arbitrator as aforesaid within twenty (20) days following receipt of the documents concerned from the Exchange, it is agreed that the said other party shall thereby be deemed to have accepted and appointed as its own arbitrator the one appointed by the party demanding arbitration, and the arbitration shall proceed forthwith before this sole arbitrator who alone, in such event, shall constitute the Arbitration Board.

The award made by the sole arbitrator or by the majority of the three (3) arbitrators, as the case may be, shall be final and binding upon the parties hereto. If the majority of the three (3) arbitrators is not obtained, then the decision of the third arbitrator shall be final and binding upon the parties hereto.

Notwithstanding the preceding provisions of this Paragraph, it is recognized that in the event of any dispute or difference of opinion arising in regard to the constructions of the VESSEL, her machinery or equipment, or concerning the quality of materials or workmanship thereof or thereon, such dispute may be referred to the Classification Society upon mutual agreement of the parties hereto as far as the Classification Society agrees to determine such dispute. The decision of the Classification Society shall be final and binding upon the parties hereto.

2. Notice of Award :

The award shall immediately be given to the BUYER and the BUILDER in writing or by cable confirmed in writing.

3. Expenses :

The Arbitration Board shall determine which party shall bear the expenses of the arbitration or the portion of such expenses which each party shall bear.

4. Entry in Court :

Judgement upon the award may be entered in any court having jurisdiction thereof.

5. Alteration of Delivery Date :

In the event of reference to arbitration of any dispute arising out of matters occurring prior to delivery of the VESSEL, the award may include any postponement of the Delivery Date which the Arbitration Board may deem appropriate.

ARTICLE XIII – EXPLANATION

Ship construction is a huge project with heavy investments from interested parties. Although the contract is between the builder and buyer, we have seen in previous articles that the project also involves various contractors, sub-contractors, banks etc. Hence there is always a possibility of differences and disputes arising between the concerned parties. The parties when signing the contract would like to ensure that any such disputes are to be handled smoothly and efficiently. The choice of law is also important and under which jurisdiction will be suitable for the parties to resolve the dispute. Most ship building contracts seek to resolve the disputes through Alternative Dispute Resolution (ADR), the preferred form is Arbitration.

Let us now see the provisions of the SAJ form under this article.

Proceedings

The SAJ form provides for the dispute to be resolved by arbitration between the parties. The dispute related to any matter which has arisen and related to the contract which the parties cannot settle amicably by themselves. Such dispute shall be submitted to and settled by arbitration held in Tokyo, Japan, by the Japan Shipping Exchange, Inc. (called the "Exchange") in accordance with the provisions of the Rules of Maritime Arbitration of the Exchange, except as otherwise specifically provided. The form specifically mentions Tokyo, Japan as the place for the arbitration proceeding.

The SAJ form explains in detail the further procedure to be followed. The party seeking the resolution of dispute should submit the written application for arbitration with the Exchange. It should include the statement of claim and the notice of appointment of an arbitrator alongwith written acceptance of the arbitrator appointed by the party.
The Exchange will then notify the other party alongwith such documents. The other party after receiving the documents within twenty days shall file in turn with the Exchange the notice of appointment of an arbitrator of its choice. The notice of appointment should contain also the written acceptance of the arbitrator appointed by the second party.

Both the arbitrators, one arbitrator appointed by the party submitting the dispute and the second arbitrator appointed by the other party, shall be deemed, in performance of office of arbitration, as the arbitrators appointed by the Maritime Arbitrations Commission (also called the "Commission") of the Exchange.

The Commission will appoint the third arbitrator. The third arbitrator will preside over the proceedings of the arbitration. The Commission selects this arbitrator from the Panel of Members of the Commission and in case of special need as required, it will select the arbitrator from among persons not so empaneled. The arbitrator such selected will have no concern whatsoever with the parties or in the subject of such dispute.

The three arbitrators together constitute the board of arbitration and are called the "Arbitrations Board" for the settlement of the dispute.

When the Exchange notifies the other party alongwith the documents, if the other party after receiving the documents within twenty days fails to appoint a second arbitrator, it shall be deemed that the second party has accepted and appointed the first arbitrator, who was appointed by the first party, as its own arbitrator. The arbitration shall then proceed with only this sole arbitrator who will solely constitute the Arbitration Board.

Award

The arbitration award shall be made by the majority of the three arbitrators. In case there is no majority of the three arbitrators, then the decision of the third arbitrator will be awarded. In case where there is only one arbitrator then the award shall be made by the sole arbitrator. The award as declared above shall be final and binding upon the parties to the dispute.

Where the dispute is related to the construction of the vessel or her machinery or equipment or quality of materials or workmanship, basically technical issues, then the parties to the dispute may agree upon referring the dispute to the Classification Society. If the Classification Society agrees then the dispute resolution takes place and the decision of the Classification Society shall be final and binding upon the parties.

The SAJ form also provides for the notice of arbitration award to be given immediately to the builder and the buyer, which party to bear the expenses of the arbitration and the entry in court of the award

Alteration of Delivery Date

The SAJ form provides for the alteration of the delivery date following the settlement of dispute by arbitration. It allows for the postponement of the delivery date as deemed appropriate by the Arbitration Board in case the arbitration of the dispute takes place before the delivery of the vessel.

From Indian perspective, The Arbitration and Conciliation Act, 1996 (as amended by the Arbitration and Conciliation (Amendment Act) of 2015 governs the proceedings of the arbitration matters related to domestic and international commercial arbitration that are conducted in India and also reference of foreign awards.

The Act has two important parts:

- Part I governs the proceedings of the arbitration (both domestic and international) as long as the seat of the arbitration is in India.

- Part II deals with the foreign awards.

The main reason for the 2015 Amendment was to make India a hub for commercial arbitration and to clear certain rules pertaining to international commercial arbitration. The definition of 'court' in relation to domestic arbitration is the same as the 1996 Act, whereas for the purpose of international commercial arbitration it means the 'High court' of competent jurisdiction. Certain provisions also provide for application even if the seat of arbitration is outside India unless it has been agreed to the contrary. Thus it strikes a balance between two important cases relating to arbitration, Bhatia International[31] and Bharat Aluminium[32] cases.

---

[31] Bhatia International v Bulk Trading SA, (2002) 4 SCC 105.
[32] Bharat Aluminium v Kaiser Aluminium, (2012) 9 SCC 552.

ARTICLE XIV – RIGHT OF ASSIGNMENT

Neither of the parties hereto shall assign this Contract to a third party unless prior consent of the other party is given in writing.

In case of assignment by the BUYER, such assignment shall further be subject to approval of the Japanese Government, and the BUYER shall remain liable under this Contract.

This Contract shall ensure to the benefit of and shall be binding upon the lawful successors or the legitimate assigns of the either of the parties hereto.

ARTICLE XIV – EXPLANATION

The SAJ form provides for assignment under this article. The builder or the buyer is not allowed to assign the contract to a third party without the prior consent of the other party in writing.

The form further provides that in case of assignment of the contract by the buyer, it should be approved by the Japanese Government and the buyer shall remain liable under the contract.

Each of the party would like to curtail the rights and duties of the other when it comes to right of assignment without the prior consent of the other party.

Assignment

Assignment is quite common in law of contracts. Assignment is generally the transfer of rights from one party to another.
When the parties to the contract transfer the obligations and benefits of the contract to another party it is called Contract Assignment.
When only the benefits of the contract are assigned to the other party and obligations are not, then it is called Assignment of Rights.

The assignee, the assignor and the obligor

The assignment consists of basically three parties, the assignee, the assignor and the obligor. The third party that is assigned the rights and obligations under the contract is called the assignee. This third party is not the original party to the contract. The rights and obligations pass from the assignor to the assignee. For example the benefit in ship building contract would be all the interests in the vessel as well as the insurance benefits.

The assignor is the party that has transferred the rights and obligations to the assignee. As explained earlier, the assignment of rights means that the assignor transfers only the benefits to the assignee.

The obligor is the other original party to the contract with the assignor. Obligor is the party that is bound to the assignor by the original contract. Obligor could be borrower, debtor, insurer etc. He has the duty to repay, make payment, do something or refrain from doing something as agreed upon.

The Indian Contract Act, 1872 does not specifically provide for the assignment of contract. However, section 130 of Transfer of Property Act, 1882 provides for transfer of actionable claim. It states that the transfer of an actionable claim […] shall be effected only by the execution of an instrument in writing signed by the transferor or his duly authorized agent, shall be complete and effectual upon the execution of such instruments, and thereupon all the rights and remedies of the transferor, whether by way of damages or otherwise, shall vest in the transferee, […].

The Assignment of interest under policy of marine insurance is provided in section 17 of The Marine Insurance Act, 1963. It states that where the assured assigns or otherwise parts with his interest in the subject-matter insured, he does not thereby transfer to the assignee his rights under the contract of insurance, unless there be an express or implied agreement with the assignee to that effect. It also mentions that the provisions of this section do not affect transmission of interest by operation of law.

The Assignment of marine policy is provided in section 52 of The Marine Insurance Act,1963. It provides as following:

(1) A marine policy may be transferred by assignment unless it contains terms expressly prohibiting assignment. It may by assigned either before or after loss.

(2) Where a marine policy has been assigned so as to pass the beneficial interest in such policy, the assignee of the policy is entitled to sue thereon in his own name; and the defendant is entitled to make any defence arising out of the contract which he would have been entitled to make if the suit had been brought in the name of the person by or on behalf of whom the policy was effected.

(3) A marine policy may be assigned by endorsement thereon or in other customary manner.

ARTICLE XV – TAXES AND DUTIES

1. Taxes and Duties in Japan :

The BUILDER shall bear and pay all taxes and duties imposed in Japan in connection with execution and/or performance of this Contract, excluding any taxes and duties imposed in Japan upon the BUYER'S Supplies.

2. Taxes and Duties in Japan :

The BUYER shall bear and pay all taxes and duties imposed outside Japan in connection with execution and/or performance of this Contract, except for taxes and duties imposed upon those items to be procured by the BUILDER for construction of the VESSEL.

ARTICLE XV – EXPLANATION

The construction of the vessel may put the builder as well as the buyer in significant tax liabilities. Equipment that are imported will also be liable for customs and duties. Foreign ship owners may be taxed differently as compared to domestic ship owner. A buyer must keep this important part of the contract in mind prior to sealing the contract as the total price will be significantly affected. The contract must be clear on this point as to the builder and buyer responsibility of payment of taxes and duties.
This article provides for the taxes and duties that are payable in Japan by the builder and the buyer.

Taxes and Duties payable by builder

All the taxes and duties that are imposed in Japan in relation to the execution and or performance of the shipbuilding contract, the builder shall pay such taxes and duties. This will exclude any taxes and duties that are imposed in Japan upon the buyer's supplies.

Taxes and Duties payable by buyer

All the taxes and duties that are imposed outside Japan in relation to the execution and or performance of the shipbuilding contract, the buyer shall pay such taxes and duties. This will exclude any taxes and duties that are imposed on those items that are procured by the builder for the construction of the vessel.

ARTICLE XVI – PATENTS, TRADEMARKS, COPYRIGHTS, ETC.S

1. Patents, Trademarks and Copyrights :

Machinery and equipment of the VESSEL may bear the patent number, trademarks or trade names of the manufacturers.

The BUILDER shall defend and save harmless the BUYER from patent liability or claims of patent infringement of any nature or kind, including costs and expenses for, or on account of any patented or patentable invention made or used in the performance of this Contract and also including costs and expenses of litigation, if any.

Nothing contained herein shall be construed as transferring any patent or trademark rights or copyright in equipment covered by this Contract, and all such rights are hereby expressly reserved to the true and lawful owners thereof.

The BUILDER'S warranty hereunder does not extend to the BUYER'S Supplies.

2. General Plans, Specifications and Working Drawings :

The BUILDER retains all rights with respect to the Specifications, and plans and working drawings, technical descriptions, calculations, test results and other data, information and documents concerning the design and construction of the VESSEL and the BUYER undertakes therefore not to disclose the same or divulge any information contained therein to any third parties, without the prior written consent of the BUILDER, excepting where it is necessary for usual operation, repair and maintenance of the VESSEL.

ARTICLE XVI – EXPLANATION

Most shipbuilding contract provides the indemnity to buyer for breaches in patents, trademarks, copyrights, design or other intellectual property rights by the builder.

Patents, Trademarks and Copyrights

The SAJ form under this provision of the article provides for the builder's indemnity to the buyer regarding patents, trademarks and copyrights. The machinery and equipment installed and fitted on the vessel may bear the patent number, trademarks or trade names of the manufacturers.

The wording of the form makes it clear that the builder indemnifies the buyer. The builder will protect the buyer and will defend the buyer from any liability of patent or any claims arising out of patent infringement of any nature or any kind. The builder will also be responsible for any costs and expenses for or on account of any patented or patentable invention that is made or is used in the performance of the contract and will also be responsible for any costs and expenses that arises for the litigation in this regard.

It is further provided that nothing contained in the provision shall be construed as transferring any patent or trademark rights or copyright in equipment that are covered by the contract. All such rights are expressly reserved to the true and lawful owners of the patent or trademark or copyright.

It is to be noted that the builder's warranty does not indemnify the buyer of its supplies.

General Plans, Specifications and Working Drawings

The SAJ form under this provision provides that all the rights concerning the general plans, specifications, working drawings, technical descriptions, calculations, test results and other data, information and documents concerning the design and construction of the vessel shall be retained with the builder. The buyer shall undertake not to disclose the same or divulge any information of the same to any third parties without the written consent of the builder, except where it would be necessary for the operation of the vessel as well as required for any repairs and maintenance to be carried out on the vessel.

Indian IPR laws

Patents

An invention to become patentable subject matter must meet the following criteria[33]:

- It should be novel.
- It should have inventive step or it must be non-obvious.
- It should be capable of Industrial application.
- It should not fall within the provisions of section 3 and 4 of the Patents Act 1970.

Section 3 of the *Patents Act, 1970* states what are not inventions. The following are not inventions within the meaning of this Act-
(a) an invention which is frivolous or which claims anything obviously contrary to well established natural laws;
(b) an invention the primary or intended use or commercial exploitation of which could be contrary to public order or morality or which causes serious prejudice to human, animal or plant life or health or to the environment;
(c) the mere discovery of a scientific principle or the formulation of an abstract theory or discovery of any living thing or non-living substance occurring in nature;
(d) the mere discovery of a new form of a known substance which does not result in the enhancement of the known efficacy of that substance or the mere discovery of any new property or new use for a known substance or of the mere use of a known process, machine or apparatus unless such known process results in a new product or employs at least one new reactant.

---

[33] www.ipindia.nic.in/faq-patents.htm

Explanation - For the purposes of this clause [...] shall be considered to be the same substance, unless they differ significantly in properties with regard to efficacy;

(e) a substance obtained by a mere admixture resulting only in the aggregation of the properties of the components thereof or a process for producing such substance;

(f) the mere arrangement or re-arrangement or duplication of known devices each functioning independently of one another in a known way;

(g) omitted by the *Patents (Amendment) Act*, 2002

(h) a method of agriculture or horticulture;

(i) any process for the medicinal [...].

(j) plants and animals [...];

(k) a mathematical or business method or a computer programme *per se* or algorithms;

(l) a literary [...];

(m) a mere scheme or rule or method of performing mental act or method of playing game;

(n) a presentation of information;

(o) topography of integrated circuits;

(p) an invention which in effect, is traditional knowledge or which is an aggregation or duplication of known properties of traditionally known component or components.

Section 4 of the *Patents Act, 1970* states that the Inventions relating to atomic energy are not patentable. No patent shall be granted in respect of an invention relating to atomic energy falling within sub section (1) of section 20 of the *Atomic Energy Act, 1962* (33 of 1962).

Trademarks

Section 2 (zb) of the *Trademarks Act , 1999* states that "trademark'' means a mark capable of being represented graphically and which is capable of distinguishing the goods or services of one person from those of others and may include shape of goods, their packaging and combination of colours; and

(1) in relation to Chapter XII (other than section 107), a registered trade mark or a mark used in relation to goods or services for the purpose of indicating or so as to indicate a connection in the course of trade between the goods or services, as the case may be, and some person having the right as proprietor to use the mark; and

(2) in relation to other provision of this Act, a mark used or proposed to be used in relation to goods or services for the purpose of indication or so to indicate a connection in the course of trade between the goods or services as the case may be, and some person having the right, either as proprietor or by way of permitted user, to use the mark whether with or without any indication of the identity of that person, and includes a certification trade mark or collective mark.

The Act also provides that unless the context otherwise requires, any reference

(a) to "trade mark" shall include reference to "collective mark" or "certification trade mark"

(b) to the use of mark shall be construed as a reference to the use of printed or other visual representation of the mark.

(c) To the use of a mark -

(1) in relation to goods, shall be construed as a reference to the use of the mark upon, or in any physical or in any other relation whatsoever, to such goods;

(2) in relation to services, shall be construed as a reference to the use of the mark as or as part of any statement about the availability, provision or performance of such services; [...]

The Act states that "collective mark" means a trade mark distinguishing the goods or services of members of an association of persons (not being a partnership within the meaning of the Indian Partnership Act, 1932) which is the proprietor of the mark from those of others.   An example is the association of chartered accountants, naval architects etc.

The Act states that "certificate trade mark" means a mark capable of distinguishing the goods or services in connection with which it is used in the course of trade which are certified by the proprietor of the mark in respect of origin, material, mode of manufacture of goods or performance of services quality, accuracy or other characteristics from goods or services in the name, as proprietor of the certification trade mark, of that person. An example is the ISO standard used internationally.

Copyrights
The Copyright is governed by *The Copyright Act, 1957.*
Section 13 of the Act provides the works in which copyright subsists – original literary, dramatic, musical, artistic works, cinematograph films and sound recording. The copyright will grant protection to the creator for his works and will prevent it being copied and reproduced without his consent.
Section 14 of the Act provides meaning of copyright as the exclusive right subject to the provisions of the Act, to do or authorize the doing of any of the following acts in respect of a work or any substantial part thereof, namely -
(a) in the case of a literary, dramatic or musical work, not being a computer programme
    (1) to reproduce the work in any material form including the storing of it in any medium by electronic means;
    (2) to issue copies of the work to the public not being copies already in circulation;
    (3) to perform the work in public or communicate it to the public;

    (4) to make any cinematograph film or sound recording in respect of the work;
    (5) to make any translation of the work;
    (6) to make any adaptation of the work;
    (7) to do, in relation to ta translation or an adaptation of the work, any of the acts specified in relation to the work in sub-clauses (1) to (6) [...]

Section 15 of the Act provides for special provision regarding copyright in designs registered or capable of being registered under *The Designs Act, 2000.*

Designs
Section 2 (d) of the *The Designs Act, 2000* states that "design'' means only the features of shape, configuration, pattern, ornament or composition of lines or colours applied to any article whether in two dimensional or three dimensional or in both forms, by any industrial

process or means, whether manual, mechanical or chemical, separate or combined, which in the finished article appeal to and are judged solely by the eye; but does not include any mode or principle or construction or anything which is in substance a mere mechanical device, and does not include any trade mark as defined in clause (v) of sub-section (1) of section 2 of the Trade and Merchandise Marks Act, 1958 or property mark as defined in section 479 of the Indian Penal Code[34] or any artistic work as defined in clause (2) of section 2 of the Copyright Act, 1957.

---

[34] Section 479 of IPC provides for Property mark – A mark used for denoting that movable property belongs to a particular person is called a property mark.

ARTICLE XVII – BUYER'S SUPPLIES

1. Responsibility of BUYER :

(a) The BUYER shall, at its own risk, cost and expense, supply and deliver to the BUILDER all of the items to be furnished by the BUYER as specified in the Specifications (herein called the "BUYER'S Supplies") at warehouse or other storage of the Shipyard in the proper condition ready for installation in or on the VESSEL, in accordance with the time schedule designated by the BUILDER.

(b) In order to facilitate installation by the BUILDER of the BUYER'S Supplies in or on the VESSEL, the BUYER shall furnish the BUILDER with necessary specifications, plans, drawings, instruction books, manuals, test reports and certificates required by the rules and regulations. The BUYER, if so requested by the BUILDER, shall, without any charge to the BUILDER, cause the representatives of the manufacturers of the BUYER'S Supplies to assist the BUILDER in installation thereof in or on the VESSEL and/or to carry out installation thereof by themselves or to make necessary adjustments thereof at the Shipyard.

(c) Any and all of the BUYER'S Supplies shall be subject to the BUILDER'S reasonable right of rejection, as and if they are found to be unsuitable or in improper condition for installation. However, if so requested by the BUYER, the BUILDER may repair or adjust the BUYER'S Supplies without prejudice to the BUILDER'S other rights hereunder and without being responsible for any consequences therefrom. In such case, the BUYER shall reimburse the BUILDER for all costs and expenses incurred by the BUILDER in such repair or adjustment and the Delivery Date shall be automatically postponed for a period of time necessary for such repair or replacement.

(d) Should the BUYER fail to deliver any of the BUYER'S Supplies within the time designated, the Delivery Date shall be automatically extended for a period of such delay in delivery. In such event, the BUYER shall be responsible for and pay to the BUILDER all losses and damages incurred by the BUILDER by reason of such delay in delivery of the BUYER'S Supplies and such payment shall be made upon delivery of the VESSEL. If delay in delivery of any of the BUYER'S Supplies exceeds thirty (30) days, then, the BUILDER shall be entitled to proceed with construction of the VESSEL without installation thereof in or on the VESSEL, without prejudice to the BUILDER'S other rights as hereinabove provided, and the BUYER shall accept and take delivery of the VESSEL so constructed.

2. Responsibility of BUILDER :

The BUILDER shall be responsible for storing and handling with reasonable care of the BUYER'S Supplies after delivery thereof at the Shipyard, and shall, at its own cost and expense, install them in or on the VESSEL, unless otherwise provided herein or agreed by the parties hereto, provided, always, that the BUILDER shall not be responsible for quality, efficiency and/or performance of any of the BUYER'S Supplies.

ARTICLE XVII – EXPLANATION

It is usual practice in shipbuilding construction for the buyer to provide its own supplies. For example, the buyer would opt to supply liferafts of its own preferred contracted company and not of the builder, similarly other LSA (life saving appliances) and FFA (fire fighting appliances) would be supplied in advance, equipment such as portable gas measuring equipments, vessel communication equipment, network computers, computer server, decorative items such as paintings, some owners even supply their own crockery. All such supplies would be kept in the builder's warehouse in the shipyard and to be fitted onboard the vessel.

The buyer must provide a list of supplies that he will be providing for the vessel.

Responsibility of BUYER

The SAJ form provides for the buyer's responsibility in regards to its supplies as following.

(a) Firstly the supplies by the buyer must be specified in the specifications of the contract. All the items must be supplied in 'proper condition' at the builder's warehouse or other storage location of the shipyard.

Supplies to be in 'proper condition' ready for installation in or on the vessel taking into consideration the time schedule of the vessel construction as designated by the builder. It is the responsibility of the buyer to supply and deliver all such items to the builder at its own risk, cost and expense.

(b) The next step after having received the buyer's supplies at the builder's warehouse or other storage location of the shipyard is the installation of such supplies.

For the builder to be able to install the items as supplied by the buyer, it will require the buyer to provide the necessary specifications, plans, drawings, instruction manuals, instruction books, test reports of the equipment and the certificates as required by rules and regulations. It is to be noted that the classification society will be involved for the prior approval of such equipments intended to be installed on the vessel in compliance of rules and regulations for the vessel type, trade, area of trading etc.

If the builder requests the buyer for seeking assistance by the representatives of the manufacturers of the items supplied by the buyer for the installation of items in or on the vessel and to carry out the installation by themselves or to make necessary adjustments at the shipyard, then the buyer shall provide such assistance at no extra cost to the builder.

(c) As explained above the supplies by the buyer are to be in 'proper condition' ready for installation in or on the vessel taking into consideration the time schedule of the vessel construction as designated by the builder. If such supplies are found to be unsuitable or in improper condition for installation in or on the vessel, then the builder has the right to reject the item or all the items. In case the supplies are found to be unsuitable or in improper condition, and the buyer requests the builder to repair or adjust the buyer's supplies then the builder may carry out the repair or adjust the buyer's supplies without prejudice to its other rights and without being held responsible for any consequences for such repair or adjustment.

All the expenses and costs for carrying out of the repair or adjustment of the buyer's supplies by the builder shall be reimbursed by the buyer. The delivery date if effected by such repair or adjustment of the buyer's supplies shall be automatically postponed for the time period required for such repair or replacement.

(d) It is the buyer's responsibility to ensure that its supplies are delivered in time at the builder's warehouse or other storage location of the shipyard taking into consideration the time schedule of the vessel construction as designated by the builder.

If the buyer does not deliver its supplies to the builder in the time frame given, then the delivery date of the vessel shall be automatically extended for a period of such delay in delivery of the supplies.
In such case the buyer will be responsible for all the losses and damages that the builder incurs due to the delay in delivery of the buyer's supplies. The buyer will pay for the losses and damages to the builder upon delivery of the vessel.

The SAJ form also provides some advantage to the builder for the delay in buyer's supplies. Where the delay in delivery of the supplies by the buyer exceeds thirty days, then the builder shall go ahead with the construction of the vessel without installing such supplies in or on the vessel, and the buyer shall accept and take delivery of the vessel so constructed without installation of its delayed supplies.

Responsibility of BUILDER

As the buyer is investing a huge amount in its supplies and arranging the logistics to ensure it reaches in 'proper condition' to the location as designated by the builder in the given time frame, the buyer will require for it supplies to be well taken care of. The SAJ form provides that the builder will be responsible for the storing and handling of the buyer's supplies with reasonable care.
Further, the buyer's supplies will be installed in or on the vessel by the builder at its own cost and expense, unless otherwise agreed by the parties.
The builder will not be responsible for the quality, efficiency and performance of the buyer's supplies.

ARTICLE XVIII – NOTICE

1. Address :

Any and all notices and communications in connection with this Contract shall be addressed as follows:

To the BUYER :

....

....

....

   Cable Address: ....

   Telex No.:   ....

To the BUILDER :

....

....

....

   Cable Address: ....

   Telex No.:   ....

2. Language :

Any and all notices and communications in connection with this Contract shall be written in the English language.

ARTICLE XVIII – EXPLANATION

We have seen in previous articles that notice needs to be sent to one party by the other and vice versa for different reasons described therein. In this article the SAJ form provides for the address of each party to the contract for all notices and communications that are required in performance of the contract.

The form also makes it clear that the notices and communication shall be written in English language.

It is usual that a given time frame is given for the notice to be served as well as for the notice to be replied by the receiver.

Let us now take a look at some of the notices that are required under Indian laws.

Section 138 of *The Negotiable Instruments Act, 1881* provides that where any cheque drawn by a person on an account maintained by him with a banker for payment of any amount of money to another person from out of that account for the discharge, in whole or in part, of any debt or other liability, is returned by the bank unpaid, either because of the amount of money standing to the credit of that account is insufficient to honour the cheque or that it exceeds the amount arranged to be paid from that account by an agreement made with that bank, such person shall be deemed to have committed an offence and shall, without prejudice to any other provisions of this Act, be punished with imprisonment for a term which may be extended to two years, or with fine which may extend to twice the amount of the cheque, or with both[…]

Section 93 of *The Negotiable Instruments Act, 1881* provides for by and to whom notice should be given. It states that when a promissory note, bill of exchange or cheque is dishonoured by non-acceptance or non-payment, the holder thereof, or some party thereto who remains liable thereon, must give notice that the instrument has been so dishonoured to all other parties whom the holder seeks to make severally liable thereon, and to some one of several parties whom he seeks to make jointly liable thereon. Nothing in this section renders it necessary to give notice to the maker of the dishonoured promissory note, or the drawee or acceptor of the dishonoured bill of exchange or cheque.

Section 94 of the Act[35] provides for the mode in which notice may be given. It states that notice of dishonour may be given to a duly authorized agent or the person to whom it is required to be given, or, where he has died, to his legal representative, or, where he has been declared an insolvent, to his assignee; may be oral or written; may, if written, be sent by post; and may be in any form; but it must inform the party to whom it is given, either in express terms or by reasonable intendment that the instrument has been dishonoured, and in what way, and that he will be held liable thereon; and it must be given within a reasonable time after dishonour, at the place of business or in case such party has no place of business at the residence of the party for whom it is intended. If the notice is duly directed and sent by post and miscarries, such miscarriage does not render the notice invalid.

---

[35] The Negotiable Instruments Act, 1881

ARTICLE XIX – EFFECTIVE DATE OF CONTRACT

This Contract shall become effective as from the date of execution hereof by the BUYER and the BUILDER.

However, in the event that Export Licence and Construction Permit for the VESSEL shall not have been issued by the Japanese Government with ………………(……….) days from the date of this Contract, then, in such case, this Contract shall automatically become null and void, unless otherwise mutually agreed in writing between the parties hereto, and both parties hereto shall be immediately and completely discharged from all of their obligations to each other under this Contract as though this Contract had never been entered into at all.

ARTICLE XIX – EXPLANATION

As per the SAJ form the effective date of the contract will be from the date of execution of the contract by the buyer and the builder.

It is to be noted, in contract laws, usually, if there is no mention of the effective date of the contract, then the contract becomes binding when it is signed. Also the effective date of the contract is not necessary to be the same as the execution date. The effective date could be earlier or later than the execution date.

Such clause in the contract sets the date when the rights and duties of the parties to the contract becomes operational.

Each of the buyer and the builder may, for a variety of reasons, be unable or unwilling to commit himself unconditionally to the contract at the time of its signature. The terms of the agreement may, for example, have to be approved formally by each party's board of directors. The parties may also need to secure bank financing to meet either the costs of construction or the contract price. Perhaps most importantly, the law governing the contract or applying at the shipyard may stipulate that a governmental approval or licence is required for the construction or export of the vessel. Such requirements may, however, be difficult or impossible to secure unless and until the project is defined and documented. It is accordingly very common for shipbuilding contracts to incorporate so-called ''Effective Date'' provisions under which either the agreement itself or the performance of obligations arising thereunder are expressly made conditional upon the occurrence of certain defined events. This structure permits each of the parties to make the necessary arrangements to permit performance of the contract without incurring a liability to the other party if its efforts should be unsuccessful, but in the knowledge that, if both parties succeed, the agreement provisionally concluded between them will become (or remain) fully binding and effective.[36]

The form also provides that if the Export Licence and Construction Permit for the vessel is not issued by the Japanese Government within agreed number of days from the date of the contract, then the contract shall become automatically null and void unless it is otherwise agreed by the parties. The parties will be discharged of all their obligations to each other.

In *Re Anglo-Russian Merchant Traders and John Batt & Co. (London) Ltd* (1917), where the export to Russia of certain metals required a UK Government permit, the sellers were held not liable in damages for their failure to supply, although they had not even applied for the permit. Their contractual obligation was only to use reasonable efforts to obtain the same and the court found as a fact that an application, even if made, would have been refused.[37]

---

[36] Curtis Simon; The Law of Shipbuilding Contracts, Fourth edition, Informa Law from Routledge, Oxon. U.K., 2012, p. 263.
[37] Ibid at p. 264.

ARTICLE XX – INTERPRETATION

1. Laws Applicable :

The parties hereto agree that the validity and interpretation of this Contract and of each Article and part thereof shall be governed by the laws of the country where the VESSEL is built.

2. Discrepancies :

All general language or requirements embodied in the Specifications are intended to amplify, explain and implement the requirements of this Contract. However, in the event that any language or requirements so embodied permit of an interpretation inconsistent with any provisions of this Contract, then, in each and every such event, the applicable provisions of this Contract shall prevail and govern. The Specifications and Plan are also intended to explain each other, and anything shown on the Plan and not stipulated in the Specifications or stipulated in the Specifications and not shown on the Plan shall be deemed and considered as if embodied in both. In the event of conflict between the Specifications and Plan, the Specifications shall prevail and govern.

3. Entire Agreement :

This Contract contains the entire agreement and understanding between the parties hereto and supersedes all prior negotiations, representations, undertakings and agreements on any subject matter of this Contract.

ARTICLE XX – EXPLANATION

One of the most important clauses in any contract is the clause concerning the laws that would be applicable in case of any dispute. The law that will be used to determine the rights and obligations of the parties to the contract.

Many newbuildings are ordered to the Asian shipyards by foreign buyers. The question that arises is that which laws will be applicable given that the parties belong to different jurisdictions, depending where the contract is signed and is to be performed, the place of business of both the parties, where the payment will be done, the currency of the payment, nationality of the parties etc.

Thus, to overcome any issues, the parties are free to select the law that will govern the contract. It is also called the Principle of Party Autonomy as the choice of laws rule in contract. However such freedom cannot be unlimited and it must be limited. The limitation is that the choice of law must not be against the *ordre public* (public policy- social, moral, economic) of the *lex fori* (law of the country where the action is sought).

Let us take a look at some of the important Conventions.

The Hague Conference on Private International law
Principles on Choice of Law in International Commercial Contracts[38]

Introduction

I.1 When parties enter into a contract that has connections with more than one State, the question of which set of legal rules governs the transaction necessarily arises. The answer to this question is obviously important to a court or arbitral tribunal that must resolve a dispute between the parties but it is also important for the parties themselves, in planning the transaction and performing the contract, to know the set of rules that governs their obligations.

I.2 Determination of the law applicable to a contract without taking into account the expressed will of the parties to the contract can lead to unhelpful uncertainty because of differences between solutions from State to State. For this reason, among others, the concept of "party autonomy" to determine the applicable law has developed and thrived.

I.3 Party autonomy, which refers to the power of parties to a contract to choose the law that governs that contract, enhances certainty and predictability within the parties primary contractual arrangement and recognizes that parties to a contract may be in the best position to determine which set of legal principles is most suitable for their transaction. Many States have reached this conclusion and, as a result, giving effect to party autonomy is the predominant view today. However, this concept is not yet applied everywhere. […]

I.6 The parties choice of law must be distinguished from the terms of the parties primary contractual arrangement ("main contract"). […]

I.7 Choice of law agreements should also be distinguished from "jurisdiction clauses" (or agreements), "forum selection clauses" (or agreements) or "choice of court clauses" (or agreements), all of which are synonyms for the parties agreement on the forum (usually a court) that will decide their dispute. Choice of law agreements should also be distinguished from "arbitration clauses" (or agreements), that denote the parties agreement to submit their dispute to an arbitral tribunal. […]

The purpose of Article 1 is to determine the scope of application of the Principles. These principles apply to choice of law in international contracts where each party is acting in the exercise of its trade or profession. A contract is international unless each party has its establishment in the same State or have such relationship, regardless of the chosen law, connected only with that State.

Article 2 establishes the parties freedom to choose the law governing their contract. Further, the law may be applicable to the whole contract or to only part of it and different laws may be applicable for different parts of the contract. However, it should be noted that certain restrictions on party autonomy are necessary and thus it provides for limitation by overriding mandatory rules and public policy as provided in Article 11.

Article 9 provides for the scope of the chosen law. It shall govern all aspects of the contract between the parties, including but not limited to the following-

a) Interpretation;

---

[38] https://www.hcch.net/en/instruments/conventions/full-text/?cid=135

b) Rights and obligations arising from the contract;
c) Performance and the consequences of non-performance, including the assessment of damages;
d) The various ways of extinguishing obligations, and prescription and limitation periods;
e) Validity and the consequences of invalidity of the contract;
f) Burden of proof and legal presumptions;
g) Pre-contractual obligations.

The 1980 Rome Convention on the Law applicable to Contractual Obligations[39]

Article 3 – Freedom of choice
1. A contract shall be governed by the law chosen by the parties. The choice must be expressed or demonstrated with reasonable certainty by the terms of the contract or the circumstances of the case. By their choice the parties can select the law applicable to the whole or a part only of the contract.
2. The parties may at any time agree to subject the contract to a law other than that which previously governed it […].
3. The fact that the parties have chosen a foreign law, whether or not accompanied by the choice of a foreign tribunal, shall not, where all the other elements relevant to the situation at the time of the choice are connected with one country only, prejudice the application of rules of the law of that country which cannot be derogated from by contract, hereinafter called "mandatory rules".
4. The existence and validity of the consent of the parties as to the choice of the applicable law shall be determined in accordance with the provisions of Articles 8, 9, and 11.

Article 4 – Applicable law in the absence of choice
1. To the extent that the law applicable to the contract has not been chosen in accordance with article 3, the contract shall be governed by the law of the country with which it is most closely connected. Nevertheless, a severable part of the contract which has a closer connection with another country may by way of exception be governed by the law of that other country.
2. Subject to the provisions of paragraph 5 of this Article, it shall be presumed that the contract is most closely connected with the country where the party who is to effect the performance which is characteristic of the contract has, at the time of conclusion of the contract, his habitual residence, or, in the case of a body corporate or unincorporated, its central administration. However, if the contract is entered into in the course of that party's trade or profession, that country shall be the country in which the principal place of business is situated or, where under the terms of the contract the performance is to be effected through a place of business other than the principal place of business, the country in which that other place of business is situated.
3. Notwithstanding the provisions of paragraph 2 of this Article, to the extent that the subject matter of the contract is a right in immovable property or a right to use immovable property it shall be presumed that the contract is most closely connected with the country where the immovable property is situated.

---

[39] www.jus.uio.no/lm/ec.applicable.law.contracts.1980/

4. A contract for the carriage of goods shall not be subject to the presumption in paragraph 2. […]
5. Paragraph 2 shall not apply if the characteristic performance cannot be determined, and the presumptions in paragraphs 2, 3 and 4 shall be disregarded if it appears from the circumstances as a whole that the contract is more closely connected with another country.

Article 10 – Scope of the applicable law
1. The law applicable to a contract by virtue of Articles 3 to 6 and 12 of this Convention shall govern in particular:
   (a) Interpretation;
   (b) Performance;
   (c) Within the limits of the powers conferred on the court by its procedural law, the consequences of breach, including the assessment of damages in so far as it is governed by rules of law;
   (d) The various ways of extinguishing obligations, and prescription and limitation of actions;
   (e) The consequences of nullity of the contract.
2. In relation to the manner of performance and the steps to be taken in the event of defective performance regard shall be had to the law of the country in which performance takes place.

The United Nations Convention on Contracts for the International Sale of Goods, 1980[40]
Explanatory Note by the UNCITRAL Secretariat on the United Nations Convention on Contracts for the International Sale of Goods
Part One. Scope of application and general provisions

Scope of application provides that the articles on scope of application indicate both what is covered by the Convention and what is not covered. The Convention applies to contracts of sale of goods between parties whose places of business are in different States and either both of those States are Contracting States or the rules of private international law lead to the law of a Contracting State. A few States have availed themselves of the authorization in article 95 to declare that they would apply the Convention only in the former and not in the latter of these two situations. As the Convention becomes more widely adopted, the practical significance of such declaration will diminish. Finally, the Convention may also apply as the law applicable to the contract if so chosen by the parties. In that case, the operation of the Convention will be subject to any limits on contractual stipulations set by the otherwise applicable law.
Party autonomy is provided as the basic principle of contractual freedom in the international sale of goods and is recognized by the provision that permits the parties to exclude the application of this Convention or derogate from or vary the effect of any of its provisions.

---

[40] https://www.uncitral.org/pdf/english/texts/sales/cisg/V1056997-CISG-e-book.pdf

This exclusion will occur, for example, if parties choose the law of a non-contracting State or the substantive domestic law of a contracting State as the law applicable to the contract. Derogation from the Convention will occur whenever a provision in the contract provides a different rule from that found in the Convention.

Let us now discuss the SAJ form provisions under the Article XX.

Laws Applicable

Under this provision it is expressed that the validity and interpretation of the contract and all of its articles and parts shall be governed by the laws of the country where the vessel is constructed. This would mean that the laws of Japan would be applied for the interpretation and validity of the contract and its provisions and parts. This is in line with the conventions discussed above.

Discrepancies

The clause reflects the scope of the specification as it is to amplify and explain as well as implement the requirement of the contract. Where the language or requirement as embodied in the specification is inconsistent with the provision of the contract, then the provision of the contract will be superior to the specification. For the purpose of interpretation the provision of the contract will be applied and shall prevail and govern.

In this clause the discrepancy between the specification and plan is also clarified. It is mentioned that the intention of the specifications and the plan are to explain each other, basically they compliment each other. If anything is shown on the plan and not in the specification or vice versa, then it will be deemed and considered that it is embodied in both. In case of any conflict between the specifications and the plan, the specifications shall prevail over the plan and govern.

Entire Agreement

This clause stipulates that the entire agreement and understanding between the builder and buyer is contained in the contract. The contract between the parties supersedes all prior negotiations, representations, undertakings and agreements on any subject matter of the contract.

Majority of contracts contain such clause. It is also sometimes referred to whole agreement clause. The purpose of this clause is to make it clear that this written contract is what is agreed between the parties and it constitutes the whole agreement. It seeks to prevent the parties from relying any preceding negotiations, pre-contract representations, undertakings and agreements, either oral or written, that have not been set out in the contract.

ARTICLE XXI – SUNDRY PROVISIONS

It is hereby mutually confirmed that the Contract Price includes the expenses amounting to Japanese Yen.....................for design and supply of drawings as the technical services required to be rendered by the BUILDER under this Contract.

   IN WITNESS WHEREOF, the parties hereto have caused this Contract to be duly executed the day and year first above written.

BUYER :   BUILDER :

....

....

....

....

By : ....   By :

....

Title : ....   Title :

....

WITNESS :   WITNESS :

By : ....   By :

....

                    Date : ...., 19.....................

ARTICLE XXI – EXPLANATION

This Article provides that the contract price includes the expenses, an amount agreed by the parties. The expense is for the design and supply of drawings as part of the technical services that are required to be rendered by the builder under the contract.

GUARANTEE

In consideration of your executing a certain Shipbuilding Contract dated……………………………, 19………………(herein called the "Contract") with

………

……………………………………..,…………,……………………………………………..(herein called the "BUYER") for construction and sale of one(1) single screw…………………………having your Hull No. ……………(herein called the "VESSEL") providing among other things for payment of the Contract Price amounting to

………………………………………………………Japanese Yen (………………..), the undersigned does hereby irrevocably and unconditionally guarantee to you, your successors and assigns due and faithful performance by the BUYER of all its liabilities and responsibilities under the Contract and any supplement, amendment, change or modification hereafter made thereto, including but not limited to, due and prompt payment of the Contract Price by the BUYER to you, your successors and assigns under the Contract and any supplement, amendment, change or modification thereto as aforesaid (hereby expressly waiving notice of any such supplement, amendment, change or modification as may be agreed to by the BUYER and confirming that this Guarantee shall be fully applicable to the Contract as so supplemented, amended, changed or modified).

Witness   Guarantor

……………………………………………………………………

……………………………………………………………………

Disclaimer

Made in the USA
Middletown, DE
12 June 2022

67035990R00060